Hometown COOKING

Volume 7
Meredith₂ Consumer Marketing
Des Moines, Iowa

Family Circle® Hometown Cooking®

Meredith® **Consumer Marketing**
Vice President, Consumer Marketing: Janet Donnelly
Consumer Marketing Product Director: Heather Sorensen
Consumer Marketing Product Manager: Wendy Merical
Business Director: Ron Clingman
Senior Production Manager: Al Rodruck

Waterbury Publications, Inc.
Editorial Director: Lisa Kingsley
Associate Editor: Tricia Bergman
Contributing Writer: Lisa Kingsley
Creative Director: Ken Carlson
Associate Design Director: Doug Samuelson
Graphic Designer: Mindy Samuelson
Contributing Copy Editors: Terri Fredrickson, Peg Smith
Contributing Indexer: Elizabeth T. Parson

Family Circle® **Magazine**
Editor in Chief: Linda Fears
Creative Director: Karmen Lizzul
Food Director: Regina Ragone, M.S., R.D.
Senior Food Editor: Julie Miltenberger
Associate Food Editor: Michael Tyrrell
Assistant Food Editor: Melissa Knific
Editorial Assistant: Megan Bingham

Meredith National Media Group
President: Tom Harty

Meredith Corporation
Chairman and Chief Executive Officer: Stephen M. Lacy

In Memoriam: E.T. Meredith III (1933–2003)

Pictured on the front cover:
Peach-Mango Pie
(recipe on page 177)

Enjoy prizewinning recipes from hometown America!

Home cooks who win recipe contests and cook-offs are an enthusiastic bunch. They know what it's like to taste victory. It spurs them to dream up, make and remake a recipe until it's perfect—and to keep entering contests. The collection of recipes in this, the seventh edition of *Family Circle® Hometown Cooking®*, celebrates that great American tradition. It brings together recipes that are prized for creativity, taste, and the community they help to create—some of the very best cooking competitions across the country.

Included in the more than 150 recipes for special-occasion breakfasts, quick weeknight meals, healthy main dishes, potluck favorites that will please a crowd, is a decadent collection of everyone's favorite—desserts.

Along the way, meet some of the cooks who contributed recipes to this book. Learn a little about their recipes and about the cooks themselves—what inspires them, why they like to cook and bake, and who they love cooking for. When you taste these recipes, you'll know why they are winners.

— **The Editors**

table of contents

getting started

Nibbles and bites get the party rolling. A generous spread stands in for dinner.

PEANUT-HONEY-BACON
CRUNCHIES

Spicy Italian Meatballs

Put some hearty in your party! Serve these generous sized meatballs with cocktail forks for easy eating.

MAKES 24 servings **PREP** 25 minutes **BAKE** 30 minutes at 350°F **SLOW COOK** 4 hours (low) or 2 hours (high)

1   **egg, lightly beaten**
½   **cup fine dry bread crumbs**
¼   **cup finely chopped onion**
¼   **cup finely chopped bottled pepperoncini salad peppers**
1   **teaspoon Italian seasoning, crushed**
1   **clove garlic, minced**
1   **pound lean ground beef**
1   **pound bulk Italian sausage**
1   **28-ounce can crushed tomatoes**
½   **cup finely chopped onion (1 medium)**
1   **tablespoon balsamic vinegar**
2   **cloves garlic, minced**
½   **teaspoon dried oregano, crushed**
¼   **teaspoon crushed red pepper**
     Pepperoncini (optional)
     Parsley sprig (optional)

1 Preheat oven to 350°F. In a large bowl combine egg, bread crumbs, ¼ cup onion, pepperoncini peppers, Italian seasoning, and the 1 clove garlic; mix well. Add ground beef and sausage; mix gently until combined. Shape into twenty-four 2-inch meatballs. Place meatballs in a 15 x 10 x 1-inch baking pan. Bake for 30 minutes; drain well.

2 Meanwhile, in a 4- to 5-quart slow cooker combine crushed tomatoes, ½ cup onion, vinegar, 2 cloves garlic, oregano, and crushed red pepper. Add baked meatballs to slow cooker; stir gently to coat.

3 Cover and cook on low-heat setting for 4 to 6 hours or on high-heat setting for 2 to 3 hours. Place meatballs in a large serving bowl. If desired, garnish with a pepperoncini and a parsley sprig.

PER SERVING 133 **CAL**; 9 g **FAT** (3 g **SAT**); 36 mg **CHOL**; 237 mg **SODIUM**; 5 g **CARB**; 1 g **FIBER**; 7 g **PRO**

Georgia Peach Ribs

For even more flavor, broil the ribs (see Step 1 of the recipe on page 10) before adding them to the slow cooker and coating with the peach preserves mixture.

MAKES 12 servings **PREP** 15 minutes **SLOW COOK** 5 hours (low) or 2½ hours (high)

2½	**pounds pork loin back ribs**
1	**12-ounce jar peach preserves**
½	**cup finely chopped onion (1 medium)**
1	**tablespoon bourbon**
1	**tablespoon yellow mustard**
1	**tablespoon cider vinegar**
¼	**teaspoon salt**
¼	**teaspoon cayenne pepper**
	Cayenne pepper (optional)
	Sliced green onions (optional)

1 Cut ribs into single-rib portions. Place ribs in a 3½- or 4-quart slow cooker. In a medium bowl combine peach preserves, onion, bourbon, mustard, vinegar, salt, and cayenne pepper. Pour over ribs and toss to coat.

2 Cover and cook on low-heat setting for 5 to 6 hours or on high-heat setting for 2½ to 3 hours. Serve immediately or keep warm, covered, on warm-heat setting or low-heat setting for up to 2 hours. Use tongs to remove ribs from cooking liquid to serve. If desired, sprinkle with additional cayenne pepper and green onions.

PER SERVING 205 **CAL**; 13 g **FAT** (5 g **SAT**); 47 mg **CHOL**; 80 mg **SODIUM**; 10 g **CARB**; 0 g **FIBER**; 10 g **PRO**

Apricot Chipotle Pork Ribs

Serve these saucy, smoky, delightfully sloppy ribs with lots of napkins. If you like food on the spicier side, use two chipotle chiles in adobe sauce.

MAKES 6 servings **PREP** 20 minutes **SLOW COOK** 6 hours (low) or 3 hours (high)

3   **pounds pork loin back ribs**
     Salt
     Black pepper
½   **cup bottled chili sauce**
½   **cup apricot preserves**
2   **tablespoons packed brown sugar**
1   **to 2 chipotle chile peppers in adobo sauce, chopped***

1 Preheat broiler. Cut ribs into 1- or 2-rib portions. Sprinkle lightly with salt and black pepper. Place ribs on the rack of an unheated broiler pan. Broil ribs 5 to 6 inches from the heat about 10 minutes or until brown, turning once. Transfer ribs to a 4- to 5-quart slow cooker.

2 In a small bowl stir together chili sauce, apricot preserves, brown sugar, and chile peppers. Pour over ribs in slow cooker.

3 Cover and cook on low-heat setting for 6 to 7 hours or on high-heat setting for 3 to 3½ hours. Transfer ribs to a serving platter. Transfer sauce to a small bowl; skim fat from sauce and serve with ribs.

***Tip** Because chile peppers contain volatile oils that can burn your skin and eyes, avoid direct contact with them as much as possible. When working with chile peppers, wear plastic or rubber gloves. If your bare hands touch the peppers, wash your hands and nails well with soap and warm water.

PER SERVING 314 **CAL**; 11 g **FAT** (4 g **SAT**); 81 mg **CHOL**; 472 mg **SODIUM**; 27 g **CARB**; 2 g **FIBER**; 25 g **PRO**

Peanut-Honey-Bacon Crunchies

These crunchy bacon-wrapped water chestnuts are a take on the classic appetizer rumaki, which was popularized by Vic Bergeron—also known as Trader Vic—at his San Francisco restaurant during the tiki fad of the 1950s.

MAKES 24 servings **PREP** 25 minutes **BAKE** 12 minutes at 425°F

1   **pound thick-sliced bacon, halved crosswise**
2   **tablespoons honey**
⅓   **cup honey-roasted peanuts, finely chopped**
1   **teaspoon ground ancho chile pepper**
1   **8-ounce can whole water chestnuts, drained, and large pieces cut in half**
     Honey (optional)

1 Preheat oven to 425°F. Line two large baking sheets with foil. Arrange bacon on sheets. Bake for 7 to 9 minutes or just until bacon is browned but pliable. Drain on paper towels. Discard foil and line the baking sheets with clean foil. Place drained bacon on the clean foil.

2 Meanwhile, in a small bowl combine honey, peanuts, and chile pepper. Spoon about ½ teaspoon peanut mixture in the center of each bacon slice. Place a water chestnut half over the peanut mixture. Fold ends of bacon slices up on water chestnut pieces, overlapping in the center. Push a wooden toothpick through the bacon into water chestnuts.

3 Bake 5 minutes or until bacon is golden brown and chestnuts are heated through. If desired, drizzle with honey. Serve warm.

PER SERVING 85 **CAL**; 5 g **FAT** (2 g **SAT**); 10 mg **CHOL**; 148 mg **SODIUM**; 3 g **CARB**; 0 g **FIBER**; 3 g **PRO**

Sugared Bacon-Wrapped Smokies

Coating the bacon-wrapped sausages in brown sugar before baking gives them a crunchy glaze. The combination of sweet, smoky, and salty is irresistible!

MAKES 45 servings **PREP** 35 minutes **BAKE** 30 minutes at 350°F

	Nonstick cooking spray
1	16-ounce package small cooked smoked sausage links
15	slices bacon, each cut crosswise into thirds
¾	cup packed brown sugar

1 Preheat oven to 350°F. Line a 15 x 10 x 1-inch baking pan with foil. Lightly coat foil with cooking spray; set pan aside.

2 Wrap each sausage link with a bacon piece, overlapping bacon ends. Press ends to seal or secure with a wooden toothpick.

3 Place brown sugar in a large plastic bag. Add bacon-wrapped sausages, several at a time, shaking gently to coat. Place sausages in the prepared baking pan. If desired, cover and chill for up to 24 hours.

4 Bake, uncovered, about 30 minutes or until bacon is browned.

PER SERVING 102 **CAL**; 8 g **FAT** (3 g **SAT**); 15 mg **CHOL**; 210 mg **SODIUM**; 4 g **CARB**; 0 g **FIBER**; 3 g **PRO**

Stuffed Mushrooms with Lemon-Pea Hummus

If you can't find fresh garden peas, substitute 1 cup of frozen peas for the fresh peas with virtually no difference in taste or texture. Cook them for the minimum time—just 2 minutes—before adding to the ice water.

MAKES 12 servings **PREP** 25 minutes **BAKE** 13 minutes at 425°F

12	large fresh mushrooms (1½ to 2 inches in diameter)
	Nonstick cooking spray
1	cup shelled fresh English peas (1 pound in pods)
2	tablespoons olive oil
½	teaspoon finely shredded lemon peel
1	tablespoon lemon juice
1	to 2 teaspoons snipped fresh mint
1	tablespoon chopped fresh spring garlic*
	Salt and black pepper
2	tablespoons grated Parmigiano-Reggiano cheese
	Pea shoots or small fresh mint leaves (optional)

1 Preheat oven to 425°F. Clean mushrooms. Remove stems from mushrooms; discard stems or save for another use. Place mushroom caps, stem sides down, in a 15 x 10 x 1-inch baking pan. Lightly coat the rounded side of each mushroom cap with cooking spray. Bake for 5 minutes. Carefully place mushroom caps, stem sides down, on a double thickness of paper towels to drain while preparing filling. Set pan aside.

2 For hummus, fill a medium saucepan half full of water. Bring to boiling. Add peas and cook for 2 to 3 minutes or just until tender. Drain and quickly add to a large bowl of ice water to cool quickly. Drain peas well. Place ¾ cup of the peas in a blender or food processor. Add olive oil, lemon peel, lemon juice, and 1 to 2 teaspoons mint. Cover and blend or process until almost smooth. Transfer hummus to a medium bowl. Stir in the remaining peas and the spring garlic. Season with salt and pepper.

3 Spoon hummus into mushroom caps. Arrange the stuffed mushroom caps in the baking pan. Sprinkle with cheese. Bake 8 minutes or until heated through and cheese is melted. Serve warm or at room temperature. If desired, garnish with pea shoots or mint leaves.

***Tip** If spring garlic is not available, substitute 1 tablespoon chopped green onions and 1 clove minced garlic.

PER SERVING 40 **CAL**; 3 g **FAT** (0 g **SAT**); 1 mg **CHOL**; 39 mg **SODIUM**; 3 g **CARB**; 1 g **FIBER**; 2 g **PRO**

Mediterranean Chicken and Wild Rice Cups

Chicken and rice is a common combination, but they came together in a very special way in these bite-size appetizers created by Canadian Terri Gilson. She is the Grand Prize winner of the 2013 Chicken and Wild Rice Recipe Roundup sponsored by the USA Rice Federation, California Rice Advisory Board and National Chicken Council. "This contest was particularly fun and challenging," Terri says, "because you could only use five ingredients in addition to the core ingredients." She obviously picked the right ones. Terri won a $500 Visa gift card and an Aroma® brand ricer cooker.

MAKES 36 servings **PREP** 15 minutes **BAKE** 15 minutes at 400°F **COOL** 5 minutes

	Nonstick cooking spray
3	**eggs, lightly beaten**
2	**cups cooked shredded chicken breast**
2	**cups cooked brown rice**
1	**cup cooked wild rice**
1	**cup crumbled feta cheese**
⅔	**cup sliced pitted ripe olives**
⅓	**cup oil-packed dried tomatoes, drained and finely chopped**
2	**teaspoons olive oil**
3	**cloves garlic, minced**
	Tzatziki Sauce (optional)

1 Preheat oven to 400°F. Lightly grease thirty-six 1¾-inch muffin cups; set aside. In a large bowl combine eggs, chicken, rices, Feta cheese, olives, dried tomatoes, oil, and garlic; mix well.

2 Lightly press about 1½ tablespoons of the chicken-rice mixture into each cup, filling to just below the rim. Bake for 15 to 20 minutes or until lightly browned. Cool in muffin cups on a wire rack for 5 minutes. Remove from muffin cups. Serve warm with Tzatziki Sauce, if desired.

Tzatziki Sauce In a small bowl combine one 6-ounce carton plain Greek or regular yogurt; 1 cup shredded, seeded cucumber; 1 tablespoon lemon juice; 1 tablespoon olive oil; 1 tablespoon snipped fresh mint; 1 clove garlic, minced; and ¼ teaspoon salt. Serve immediately or cover and chill for up to 4 hours. Makes 1½ cups.

PER SERVING 49 **CAL**; 2 g **FAT** (1 g **SAT**); 23 mg **CHOL**; 72 mg **SODIUM**; 4 g **CARB**; 0 g **FIBER**; 4 g **PRO**

Toasted Baguette with Herbed Butter and Radishes

The classic French hors d'oeuvre of radishes, butter, and salt gets a flavor boost from fresh herbs in this recipe. Make it in spring, when radishes are in season and at their crisp sweet-and-peppery best.

MAKES 8 servings **PREP** 20 minutes
BAKE 4 minutes at 425°F

- ½ **cup unsalted butter, softened**
- 2 **tablespoons finely chopped green onion (1)**
- 1 **tablespoon snipped fresh basil**
- 2 **teaspoons snipped fresh parsley**
- 1 **teaspoon snipped fresh thyme**
- 1 **teaspoon finely shredded lemon peel**
- ⅛ **teaspoon freshly ground black pepper**
- 8 **ounces baguette-style French bread, diagonally sliced ¼ inch thick**
- 2 **bunches assorted radishes with stems**
- 2 **teaspoons coarse sea salt or smoked sea salt**
  Coarse sea salt or smoked sea salt (optional)

1 Preheat oven to 425°F. In a medium bowl stir together butter, green onion, basil, parsley, thyme, lemon peel, and pepper. Set aside.

2 Arrange bread slices on a baking sheet. Bake for 4 to 5 minutes or until lightly toasted, turning once. Allow bread to cool. Spread cooled toasts with herbed butter. Arrange bread slices on a platter. Set aside.

3 Stem and thinly slice about five radishes; you should have about ¾ cup. Just before serving, top bread slices with sliced radishes. Add the remaining radishes to the platter. Sprinkle toasts with salt. If desired, serve with a small bowl of sea salt for dipping whole radishes.

PER SERVING 180 **CAL**; 12 g **FAT** (7 g **SAT**); 31 mg **CHOL**; 591 mg **SODIUM**; 16 g **CARB**; 1 g **FIBER**; 3 g **PRO**

Antipasto Platter with Tomato Chutney

For the prettiest presentation, look for the 1-inch balls of fresh mozzarella called bocconcini—or the even smaller ones, called pearls.

MAKES 10 servings **PREP** 30 minutes **COOK** 30 minutes
COOL 20 minutes

- 2 **pounds roma tomatoes, seeded and coarsely chopped**
- 1 **medium onion, finely chopped**
- 2 **cloves garlic, minced**
- ½ **cup red wine vinegar**
- 1 **tablespoon sugar**
- ½ **teaspoon salt**
- ½ **teaspoon paprika**
- ⅛ **to ¼ teaspoon cayenne pepper**
- 1 **tablespoon snipped fresh basil**
  Antipasto:
  Blanched asparagus and broccoli
  Fresh mozzarella
  Baby sweet peppers
  Paper thin slices prosciutto
  Flaxseed or other crackers or breads

1 For the tomato chutney, in a medium saucepan combine tomatoes, onion, garlic, vinegar, sugar, salt, paprika, and cayenne pepper. Bring to boiling; reduce heat. Simmer, uncovered, for 30 minutes or until mixture is thickened and saucelike, stirring occasionally. Remove from heat; cool about 20 minutes. Place in a serving bowl and sprinkle with basil.

2 Place desired antipasto ingredients on a serving plate. Serve with tomato chutney.

PER SERVING CHUTNEY 29 **CAL**; 0 g **FAT**; 0 g **CHOL**; 122 mg **SODIUM**; 6 g **CARB**; 1 g **FIBER**; 0 g **FIBER**; 1 g **PRO**

ANTIPASTO PLATTER
WITH TOMATO CHUTNEY

Baked Santa Fe Dip

For a fresh crunch, serve cool and crisp vegetables such as sweet pepper strips and sliced jicama to dunk into this warm cheesy dip.

MAKES 28 servings **PREP** 20 minutes **BAKE** 25 minutes at 350°F

2 cups shredded cheddar cheese (8 ounces)

1 cup shredded Monterey Jack or mozzarella cheese (4 ounces)

½ cup light mayonnaise dressing or salad dressing

1 8-ounce can whole kernel corn, drained (¾ cup)

1 4-ounce can chopped green chili peppers, drained

2 teaspoons finely chopped canned chipotle chili peppers in adobo sauce (see tip, page 10)

¼ teaspoon garlic powder

1 medium tomato, seeded and chopped (¾ cup)

¼ cup sliced green onion

2 tablespoons snipped fresh cilantro

Vegetables such as sweet pepper wedges and sliced jicama

Lightly salted tortilla chips or baked tortilla wedges

1 Preheat oven to 350°F. In a large bowl stir together cheeses, mayonnaise, corn, green chili peppers, chipotle peppers, and garlic powder. Spread mixture into a shallow 1-quart casserole or 9-inch pie plate. In a small bowl combine tomato, green onion, and cilantro; set aside.

2 Bake dip for 25 minutes or until heated through. Spoon tomato mixture in the center. Serve warm with vegetables and tortilla chips.

PER SERVING 69 **CAL**; 5 g **FAT** (3 g **SAT**); 12 mg **CHOL**; 137 mg **SODIUM**; 2 g **CARB**; 0 g **FIBER**; 3 g **PRO**

Lemony Artichoke Dip

Fresh lemon juice and peel add brightness to this creamy classic—and perennially popular—warm artichoke dip.

MAKES 32 servings **PREP** 25 minutes **SLOW COOK** 2 hours (low)

1	**tablespoon olive oil**
1	**cup chopped fresh mushrooms**
¼	**cup chopped red sweet pepper**
3	**tablespoons finely chopped shallot**
1	**clove garlic, minced**
1	**8-ounce carton sour cream**
½	**cup original cream cheese for cooking**
1	**teaspoon finely shredded lemon peel**
1	**tablespoon lemon juice**
1	**tablespoon Dijon mustard**
3	**6-ounce jars marinated artichoke hearts, drained and coarsely chopped**
1	**cup shredded Gruyère or Swiss cheese (4 ounces)**
	Fresh snipped parsley (optional)
	Lemon wedges (optional)
	Toasted baguette-style French bread slices or pita chips

1 In a medium skillet heat oil over medium heat. Add mushrooms, sweet pepper, shallot, and garlic; cook mixture until pepper and shallot are tender, stirring frequently.

2 In a medium bowl combine sour cream, cream cheese for cooking, lemon peel, lemon juice, and mustard. Stir in mushroom mixture, artichoke hearts, and Gruyère cheese. Spoon artichoke dip into a 1½- or 2-quart slow cooker.

3 Cover and cook on low-heat setting for 2 to 2½ hours or until heated through. Serve immediately or keep warm, covered, on warm-heat or low-heat setting for up to 2 hours. Stir before serving. If desired, garnish with parsley and/or lemon wedges. Serve with toasted bread slices or pita chips.

PER SERVING 71 **CAL**; 6 g **FAT** (2 g **SAT**); 9 mg **CHOL**; 105 mg **SODIUM**; 2 g **CARB**; 0 g **FIBER**; 2 g **PRO**

Hot Wing Dip

Chicken wings are swapped out for lean breast meat in this Buffalo-style dip. To make it, you'll need a mini (1½-quart) slow cooker. If you don't have one, they're inexpensive to buy and a handy size to have for entertaining.

MAKES 10 servings **PREP** 15 minutes **SLOW COOK** 3 hours (low)

8	ounces reduced-fat cream cheese (Neufchâtel), cut up
¼	to ½ cup bottled Buffalo wing sauce
1½	tablespoons bottled reduced-calorie blue cheese salad dressing
1	cup chopped cooked chicken breast
1	stalk celery, finely chopped (½ cup)
1	fresh jalapeño, seeded and minced (see tip, page 10)
20	stalks celery, halved crosswise
	Fresh jalapeño, seeded and sliced (see tip, page 10) (optional)

1 In a 1½-quart slow cooker combine cream cheese, wing sauce, salad dressing, chicken, finely chopped celery, and jalapeño.

2 Cover and cook on low-heat setting for 3 to 4 hours. If no heat setting is available, cook for 3 hours. Serve with celery pieces. If desired, garnish dip with a few slices of jalapeño.

PER SERVING 99 **CAL**; 7 g **FAT** (3 g **SAT**); 29 mg **CHOL**; 168 mg **SODIUM**; 3 g **CARB**; 1 g **FIBER**; 7 g **PRO**

FETA, HONEY, AND DATE SPREAD

Feta, Honey, and Date Spread

This stir-together spread has it all: a balance of sweet, salty, tangy, and spicy flavors—and a creamy texture punctuated by chewy dates and crunchy toasted almonds.

MAKES 12 servings **START TO FINISH** 20 minutes

1	**cup crumbled feta (4 ounces)**
½	**cup toasted almonds,* coarsely chopped**
½	**cup pitted dates, chopped**
2	**tablespoons fresh marjoram or 1 tablespoon fresh thyme, chopped**
2	**tablespoons coarsely chopped and/or sliced green olives**
2	**teaspoons finely shredded lemon peel**
¼	**cup honey**
¼	**teaspoon cayenne pepper**
	Toasted pita bread wedges

1 In a serving bowl gently stir together feta, almonds, dates, marjoram, olives, and lemon peel. In a small microwave-safe bowl combine honey and cayenne. Warm in microwave for 15 seconds. Drizzle over spread; fold gently to combine. Serve with pita bread.

*Tip To toast whole nuts or large pieces, spread them in a shallow pan. Bake in a 350°F oven for 5 to 10 minutes, shaking the pan once or twice. Toast coconut in the same way, watching it closely to avoid burning. Toast finely chopped or ground nuts , cumin seeds, or sesame seeds in a dry skillet over medium heat. Stir often to prevent burning.

PER SERVING 168 **CAL**; 7 g **FAT** (2 g **SAT**); 8 mg **CHOL**; 286 mg **SODIUM**; 24 g **CARB**; 2 g **FIBER**; 4 g **PRO**

Brown Sugar-Cayenne Roasted Nuts

If you like a lot of spice with sweetness, increase the amount of cayenne to ¼ teaspoon.

MAKES 16 servings **PREP** 15 minutes
BAKE 35 minutes at 300°F

1	**egg white**
1	**tablespoon water**
4	**cups raw whole cashews, whole almonds, pecan halves, and/or walnut halves**
3	**tablespoons packed brown sugar**
1	**tablespoon ground cumin**
2	**teaspoons chili powder**
1	**teaspoon garlic salt**
⅛	**teaspoon cayenne pepper**

1 Preheat oven to 300°F. In a bowl combine egg white and the water; beat with a fork until frothy. Add nuts; toss to coat. Let stand for 5 minutes.

2 Meanwhile, in a large plastic bag combine brown sugar, cumin, chili powder, garlic salt, and cayenne. Add nuts; shake well to coat. Spread nuts evenly in a 15 x 10 x 1-inch baking pan.

3 Bake for 35 to 40 minutes or until nuts are toasted and coating is dry, stirring twice. Spread nuts on a large piece of foil to cool.

PER SERVING 206 **CAL**; 16 g **FAT** (3 g **SAT**); 72 mg **SODIUM**; 13 g **CARB**; 1 g **FIBER**; 7 g **PRO**

CHAPTER 2
bring on breakfast

Enticing recipes for busy weekday breakfasts or lingering weekend brunches.

DOUBLE STRAWBERRY SCONES

Spicy Brunch Lasagna

Stratas are lovely one-dish meals and this layered brunch lasagna—featuring Italian sausage, eggs, hash browns, cheese, and creamy Alfredo sauce—is truly special.

MAKES 16 servings **PREP** 40 minutes **CHILL** 8 hours **STAND** 30 minutes + 10 minutes **BAKE** 1 hour at 350°F

1½	**pounds bulk Italian sausage**
1	**24-ounce carton cottage cheese**
½	**cup finely chopped green onions (4)**
¼	**cup finely shredded carrot**
¼	**cup snipped fresh chives**
18	**eggs**
⅓	**cup milk**
½	**teaspoon salt**
½	**teaspoon black pepper**
2	**tablespoons butter**
1	**14-ounce jar Alfredo sauce**
1	**teaspoon dried Italian seasoning, crushed**
8	**no-boil lasagna noodles**
4	**cups frozen shredded hash brown potatoes, thawed**
2	**cups shredded mozzarella cheese (8 ounces)**

1 In a large skillet cook sausage over medium heat until browned; drain off fat. Set aside. Meanwhile, in a medium bowl stir together cottage cheese, green onions, carrot, and chives; set aside.

2 In an extra-large bowl whisk together eggs, milk, salt, and pepper. In a large skillet melt butter over medium heat; pour in egg mixture. Cook over medium heat, without stirring, until mixture begins to set on the bottom and around the edges. Using a spatula or a large spoon, lift and fold the partially cooked egg mixture so the uncooked portion flows underneath. Continue cooking over medium heat for 2 to 3 minutes or until egg mixture is cooked through but still glossy and moist. Immediately remove from heat.

3 In a small bowl stir together the Alfredo sauce and Italian seasoning. Spread about ½ cup of the sauce mixture on the bottom of a 3-quart rectangular baking dish. Layer half the lasagna noodles in the dish, overlapping as needed. Top with half the remaining sauce mixture, half the cottage cheese mixture, half the hash browns, half the scrambled egg mixture, and half the sausage mixture. Sprinkle with 1 cup of the cheese. Repeat layers. Cover dish tightly with plastic wrap. Refrigerate for 8 hours or overnight.

4 Before baking, let lasagna stand for 30 minutes at room temperature. Preheat oven to 350°F. Remove plastic wrap from lasagna; cover dish with foil. Bake for 45 minutes. Remove foil; bake about 15 minutes more or until heated through. Let stand for 10 minutes before serving. If desired, sprinkle with green onions.

PER SERVING 455 **CAL**; 30 g **FAT** (13 g **SAT**); 312 mg **CHOL**; 900 mg **SODIUM**; 20 g **CARB**; 1 g **FIBER**; 26 g **PRO**

Eggs Benedict Strata

All the elements of eggs Benedict—toasty bread, Canadian bacon, eggs, and rich and creamy (mock) hollandaise sauce—are present in this simple make-ahead brunch dish.

MAKES 6 servings **PREP** 30 minutes **CHILL** 2 hours **BAKE** 10 minutes at 300°F/55 minutes at 325°F **STAND** 10 minutes

8	slices whole wheat or whole grain white bread
6	cups baby spinach leaves or torn fresh kale
2	teaspoons canola oil
4	ounces Canadian-style bacon (about 7 slices), torn into bite-size pieces
4	eggs, beaten
2	egg whites, beaten
¼	cup light sour cream
2	tablespoons all-purpose flour
1	teaspoon finely shredded lemon peel
1	teaspoon dry mustard
¼	teaspoon ground black pepper
1⅔	cups fat-free milk
⅓	cup light sour cream
2	teaspoons Dijon mustard
1	to 2 tablespoons fat-free milk
	Fresh thyme sprigs (optional)

1 Preheat oven to 300°F. Place bread in a 15 x 10 x 1-inch baking pan; bake for 10 to 15 minutes or until dry, turning once. (Or, place bread slices in a single layer on a wire rack; cover loosely with a clean kitchen or paper towel and let stand 8 to 12 hours or until dried.) Tear slices into large pieces.

2 In an extra-large nonstick skillet cook spinach in hot oil over medium heat for 1 to 2 minutes or just until spinach is wilted, stirring frequently. (If using kale, cook for 6 to 8 minutes or just until tender.) Coarsely chop spinach or kale.

3 In a lightly greased 2-quart rectangular baking dish arrange half the bread pieces. Top with spinach and Canadian-style bacon. Top with remaining bread pieces.

4 In a medium bowl whisk together the eggs, egg whites, ¼ cup sour cream, flour, lemon peel, dry mustard, and black pepper. Stir in 1⅔ cups milk until well combined. Pour evenly over the layers in dish. Cover and chill for 2 to 24 hours.

5 Preheat oven to 325°F. Bake strata, uncovered, for 55 to 60 minutes or until a knife inserted near center comes out clean. Let stand for 10 minutes before serving.

6 Meanwhile, in a small bowl stir together ⅓ cup sour cream, Dijon mustard, and 1 to 2 tablespoons milk to a drizzling consistency. Drizzle sauce over strata to serve. Garnish with fresh thyme.

PER SERVING 241 **CAL**; 9 g **FAT** (3 g **SAT**); 158 mg **CHOL**; 521 mg **SODIUM**; 23 g **CARB**; 3 g **FIBER**; 17 g **PRO**

Huevos Rancheros

For additional flavor, substitute a can of fire-roasted tomatoes for the regular tomatoes.

MAKES 4 servings **START TO FINISH** 40 minutes **OVEN** 300°F

3   tablespoons olive oil or vegetable oil
9   5- to 6-inch corn tortillas
½   cup chopped onion (1 medium)
2   cloves garlic, minced
1   14.5-ounce can tomatoes, drained and cut up
1   to 2 canned chipotle chile peppers in adobo sauce, chopped, or half a 4-ounce can diced green chile peppers, drained (see tip, page 10)
2   tablespoons snipped fresh cilantro
¼   teaspoon ground cumin
8   eggs
1   tablespoon water
½   cup shredded Monterey Jack cheese or crumbled queso fresco (2 ounces)
    Fresh cilantro leaves (optional)

1 Preheat oven to 300°F. In a large skillet heat 2 tablespoons of the oil over medium-high heat. Dip tortillas, one at a time, into the oil just until hot. Drain on paper towels (do not stack), reserving oil in skillet. Keep 8 of the tortillas warm on a baking sheet in oven. Set aside the remaining tortilla.

2 For salsa, cook onion and garlic in the reserved oil for 2 to 3 minutes or until tender. Stir in tomatoes, chipotle peppers, snipped cilantro, and cumin. Bring to boiling; reduce heat. Simmer, uncovered, for 5 minutes. Transfer to a blender or food processor. Tear the reserved tortilla into pieces; add to blender or processor. Cover and blend or process until a coarse puree forms. Cover to keep warm.

3 In the same skillet heat the remaining 1 tablespoon oil over medium heat. Carefully break eggs into skillet. When whites are set and edges turn white, add the water. Cover skillet and cook eggs to desired doneness (3 to 4 minutes for soft-set yolks or 4 to 5 minutes for firm-set yolks).

4 To serve, place 1 fried egg on each warm tortilla. Top with warm salsa and sprinkle with cheese. If desired, garnish with cilantro leaves.

PER SERVING 413 **CAL**; 26 g **FAT** (7 g **SAT**); 437 mg **CHOL**; 397 mg **SODIUM**; 27 g **CARB**; 3 g **FIBER**; 20 g **PRO**

Garden-Fresh Omelets

Filled and topped with fresh-vegetable salsa featuring tomatoes, cucumber, avocado, and red onion, these light-as-air omelets are perfectly suited for breakfast or a light supper.

MAKES 4 servings **START TO FINISH** 35 minutes

1⅓ **cups coarsely chopped tomatoes, drained**
1 **cup coarsely chopped, seeded cucumber**
½ **ripe avocado, halved, seeded, peeled, and chopped**
½ **cup coarsely chopped red onion (1 medium)**
1 **clove garlic, minced**
2 **tablespoons snipped fresh parsley**
2 **tablespoons red wine vinegar**
1 **tablespoon olive oil**
2 **eggs**
1½ **cups refrigerated or frozen egg product, thawed**
¼ **cup water**
1 **tablespoon snipped fresh oregano or 1 teaspoon dried oregano, crushed**
¼ **teaspoon salt**
¼ **teaspoon black pepper**
⅛ **teaspoon crushed red pepper**
¼ **cup crumbled reduced-fat feta cheese**

1 For salsa, in a medium bowl stir together tomatoes, cucumber, avocado, onion, garlic, parsley, vinegar, and 1 teaspoon of the oil. Set aside.

2 In a medium bowl whisk together eggs, egg product, the water, oregano, salt, black pepper, and crushed red pepper. For each omelet, in a medium nonstick skillet heat ½ teaspoon of the remaining oil over medium heat. Add ½ cup of the egg mixture to skillet. Stir eggs with a spatula until mixture resembles cooked egg pieces surrounded by liquid. Stop stirring, but continue cooking until egg is set. Spoon ⅓ cup of the salsa over one side of the omelet. Keep warm while cooking remaining omelets.

3 Serve each omelet with some of the remaining salsa. and sprinkle with 1 tablespoon of the feta cheese.

PER SERVING 181 **CAL**; 10 g **FAT** (2 g **SAT**); 108 mg **CHOL**; 478 mg **SODIUM**; 9 g **CARB**; 2 g **FIBER**; 15 g **PRO**

Mediterranean Crispy Potato Breakfast Roulade

One of Wisconsin chiropractor Crystal Schmidt's favorite breakfasts is crisp-fried salami on scrambled eggs seasoned with herbs and spices. Crystal used that as her springboard to create this 1st prize-winning recipe in the 2013 Breakfast of Champions contest sponsored by the Wisconsin Vegetable & Potato Grower's Association. Her taste-testers were her mom, dad, and sister. When they gave it a hearty thumb's-up, Crystal entered it, then won a $400 gift card to Williams-Sonoma.

MAKES 3 servings **PREP** 35 minutes **BAKE** 35 minutes at 425°F

1	tablespoon olive oil
3	medium Wisconsin russet potatoes (about 1 pound), peeled
6	slices hard salami
3	eggs, lightly beaten
½	cup finely shredded Parmesan cheese
1	teaspoon dried oregano, crushed
½	teaspoon sea salt
½	teaspoon black pepper
3	cups torn mixed greens
1	tablespoon vinaigrette or salad dressing

1 Preheat the oven to 425°F. Line a large baking sheet with parchment. Evenly brush parchment with olive oil; set aside. Use a mandolin or food processor to thinly slice potatoes into circles. Arrange potatoes, shingle-fashion on the prepared baking sheet to form a 17 x 11-inch rectangle, overlapping slices by one-third. Cover with foil. Bake 5 minutes. Remove foil and bake 15 minutes, or until starting to turn brown.

2 Meanwhile, in a large skillet cook hard salami over medium heat for 3 to 5 minutes or just until it turns crisp. Remove salami from the pan and drain on paper towels. When cool enough to handle, crumble salami. Drain all but 1 teaspoon drippings from the skillet.

3 Reduce heat to medium-low. Add the eggs to the skillet. Cook for 1 to 2 minutes or until mostly set but still quite runny. Transfer to a plate.

4 Remove the potato sheet from the oven and evenly sprinkle with Parmesan cheese, oregano, salt, and pepper. Place salami in a line along an 11-inch end of the potatoes, about 1 inch from the edge. Spoon eggs evenly on top of the salami.

5 Starting at the end with the filling, gently lift the edge of the parchment paper and allow the potato sheet to form a roll around the filling. Continue to lift and roll the potato sheet around the filling to the opposite end. Bake 15 to 20 minutes or until top is golden and edges are crisp.

6 Place mixed greens on a serving platter. Toss with vinaigrette. Cut roulade into 6 pieces and serve on greens.

PER SERVING 351 **CAL**; 18 g **FAT** (6 g **SAT**); 209 mg **CHOL**; 894 mg **SODIUM**; 30 g **CARB**; 3 g **FIBER**; 18 g **PRO**

Bacon, Cheddar, and Tomato Rösti

Rösti (RAW-stee) means "crisp and golden" in Switzerland, the country of origin for these versatile potato cakes. Originally served as an accompaniment to roasted meats, they can also stand alone as the main event. This breakfast version starts with shredded hash browns (for speed) and has shredded zucchini for added nutrition and lightness.

MAKES 4 servings **PREP** 20 minutes **COOK** 14 minutes

1	egg
1	egg white
1	medium zucchini, shredded (about 1½ cups)
2	slices packaged ready-to-serve cooked bacon, crumbled
1	teaspoon snipped fresh oregano
¼	teaspoon salt
¼	teaspoon black pepper
4	cups frozen shredded or diced hash brown potatoes with onions and peppers
2	teaspoons vegetable oil
½	cup shredded reduced-fat cheddar cheese (2 ounces)
1	cup quartered cherry tomatoes
	Fresh oregano leaves

1 In a large bowl beat together whole egg and egg white. Stir in shredded zucchini, crumbled bacon, the 1 teaspoon oregano, the salt, and pepper. Stir in frozen potatoes.

2 In a large nonstick skillet heat oil over medium heat. Spread potato mixture evenly in skillet. Cook for 8 to 10 minutes or until bottom is browned. Using the edge of a nonmetal spatula, cut mixture into quarters. Carefully flip each quarter. Sprinkle with cheese. Cook about 6 minutes more or until browned on the bottom. Serve topped with tomatoes and oregano leaves.

PER SERVING 208 **CAL**; 7 g **FAT** (3 g **SAT**); 63 mg **CHOL**; 374 mg **SODIUM**; 26 g **CARB**; 4 g **FIBER**; 10 g **PRO**

Mediterranean Breakfast Sandwiches

This healthful breakfast of egg, veggies, and low-fat cheese tucked into a toasty whole-grain sandwich bun will keep you energized and satisfied until lunchtime.

MAKES 4 servings **PREP** 15 minutes **BAKE** 5 minutes at 375°F

4	**multigrain sandwich thins**
4	**teaspoons olive oil**
1	**tablespoon snipped fresh rosemary or ½ teaspoon dried rosemary, crushed**
4	**eggs**
2	**cups fresh baby spinach leaves**
1	**medium tomato, cut into 8 thin slices**
¼	**cup crumbled reduced-fat feta cheese (1 ounce)**
⅛	**teaspoon kosher salt**
	Freshly ground black pepper

1 Preheat oven to 375°F. Open sandwich thins in halves; brush cut sides with 2 teaspoons of the oil. Place on baking sheet; toast in oven about 5 minutes or until edges are light brown and crisp.

2 Meanwhile, in a large skillet heat the remaining 2 teaspoons oil and the rosemary over medium-high heat. Break eggs, one at a time, into skillet. Cook about 1 minute or until whites are set but yolks are still runny. Break yolks with spatula. Flip eggs; cook on other side until done. Remove from heat.

3 Place the bottom halves of the toasted sandwich thins on four serving plates. Divide spinach among sandwich thins on plates. Top each with 2 tomato slices, 1 egg, and 1 tablespoon of the feta cheese. Sprinkle with salt and pepper. Top with sandwich thin halves.

PER SERVING 242 **CAL**; 12 g **FAT** (3 g **SAT**); 214 mg **CHOL**; 501 mg **SODIUM**; 25 g **CARB**; 6 g **FIBER**; 13 g **PRO**

Autumn Fruit Salad

The key to this simple fall fruit salad is to make it with the best pears possible. Look for pears that are slightly soft and fragrant, with no cuts or bruises.

MAKES 4 servings   **START TO FINISH** 15 minutes

- 2   ripe pears, cubed
- 2   tablespoons lemon juice
- ⅓   cup chopped pecans, toasted (see tip, page 25)
- ¼   cup plain low-fat Greek yogurt
- 1   tablespoon honey or agave nectar
-     Ground cinnamon (optional)

1 In a medium bowl combine pears and lemon juice. Stir in pecans. Divide among four serving bowls.

2 In a small bowl combine yogurt and honey. Top each salad with some of the yogurt mixture. If desired, sprinkle with cinnamon.

PER SERVING 140 **CAL**; 7 g **FAT** (1 g **SAT**); 1 mg **CHOL**; 7 mg **SODIUM**; 20 g **CARB**; 3 g **FIBER**; 3 g **PRO**

Smoked Salmon and Melon Salad

This visually striking salad is perfect for a celebratory brunch or luncheon. Serve it with rolls, popovers, or crusty bread.

MAKES 6 servings   **START TO FINISH** 25 minutes

- 1   recipe Yogurt-Cardamom Dressing
- ⅓   cup fresh mint leaves
- 1   teaspoon finely shredded lemon peel
- ¼   teaspoon cracked black pepper
- ½   cantaloupe, peeled and cut into thin wedges (about 2 cups)
- 2   cups blueberries or seedless red grapes
- ½   honeydew melon, cut into thin wedges (about 2 cups)
- 8   ounces smoked salmon, skin and bones removed, coarsely broken
- 2   cups thinly sliced fennel

1 Prepare Yogurt-Cardamom Dressing; set aside.

2 For topping, in a small bowl combine mint, lemon peel, and pepper; set aside. In a trifle dish or straight-sided glass serving bowl layer cantaloupe, half the blueberries, honeydew melon, remaining blueberries, the salmon, and sliced fennel. Sprinkle with mint leaves topping. Serve with Yogurt-Cardamom Dressing.

Yogurt-Cardamom Dressing In a small bowl combine one 6-ounce carton plain low-fat yogurt; ¼ cup olive oil; 2 tablespoons lemon juice; 1 tablespoon honey; 1 clove garlic, minced; ½ teaspoon ground cardamon or ground nutmeg; ½ teaspoon cracked black pepper; and ¼ teaspoon salt.

PER SERVING 239 **CAL**; 12 g **FAT** (2 g **SAT**); 10 mg **CHOL**; 452 mg **SODIUM**; 26 g **CARB**; 3 g **FIBER**; 10 g **PRO**

SMOKED SALMON AND
MELON SALAD

Cinnamon Rolls

There were more than 200 entries and some very tough competition in the Iowa State Fair 2013 Cinnamon Roll contest sponsored by Tone's Spices. But Kim Grove's cinnamon rolls were anything but tough. The tender texture of the potato dough and fragrant Saigon cinnamon won the Clive, Iowa, baker first prize—a $3,000 cash prize and bragging rights for a year.

MAKES 24 servings **PREP** 45 minutes **COOK** 15 minutes **RISE** 1 hour + 45 minutes
BAKE 25 minutes at 350°F

1½	cups water
1	medium russet potato, peeled and cut into ½-inch-thick slices
1	cup buttermilk
½	cup granulated sugar
3	tablespoons butter or margarine
2	teaspoons salt
½	cup warm water
2	packages Fleishmann's® Active Dry Yeast
½	teaspoon granulated sugar
7	to 7½ cups all-purpose flour
1	cup packed brown sugar
1½	teaspoons Spice Islands® Ground Saigon Cinnamon
½	cup butter or margarine, softened
2	ounces cream cheese, softened
3	tablespoons butter, softened
⅛	teaspoon salt
2	cups powdered sugar
2	tablespoons very hot water

1 In a medium saucepan combine the 1½ cups water and the potato. Bring to a boil. Reduce heat and simmer, covered, 15 to 20 minutes or until potato is very soft; do not drain off water. Mash until smooth (a few lumps are fine). Measure mashed potato. Add additional water if needed to equal 1¾ cups. Return mashed potato to saucepan. Add buttermilk, ½ cup granulated sugar, 3 tablespoons butter, and 2 teaspoons salt. Heat or cool until mixture is warm (100° to 110°F).

2 In a small bowl combine the ½ cup warm water, the yeast, and ½ teaspoon granulated sugar. Let stand 5 to 10 minutes or until foamy.

3 In a large mixing bowl combine potato mixture, 2 cups of the flour and yeast mixture. Beat with an electric mixer on medium to high for 2 minutes or until very smooth. Gradually beat in flour, 1 cup at a time, until a soft dough forms. On a lightly floured surface knead dough for 8 to 10 minutes or until smooth and elastic. Place in a greased bowl; turn to coat. Cover and let rise in a warm, draft-free place for 1 to 1¼ hours or until doubled.

4 Punch dough down and place on a lightly floured surface. Divide dough in half. Roll each portion into a 15 x 10-inch rectangle. In a small bowl combine brown sugar and cinnamon. Spread each dough portion with ¼ cup butter then sprinkle with half the brown sugar mixture. Roll up, beginning with the long side. Seal edges. Cut into 12 rolls. Place rolls in two greased 13 x 9 x 2-inch baking pans.

5 Cover and let rise 45 to 60 minutes or until doubled. Preheat oven to 350°F. Bake for 25 to 30 minutes or until lightly browned. Cool slightly on a wire rack.

6 For icing, in a medium bowl beat cream cheese, butter, and salt with an electric mixer on medium to high for 30 seconds. Add powdered sugar and beat until blended. Gradually add water until desired consistency. Spread icing over rolls.

PER SERVING 302 **CAL**; 8 g **FAT** (5 g **SAT**); 21 mg **CHOL**; 288 mg **SODIUM**; 53 g **CARB**; 1 g **FIBER**; 5 g **PRO**

Double Strawberry Scones

Both fresh and freeze-dried strawberries are used in these pretty scones. Fresh basil is the surprising complementary flavor to the sweetness of strawberries.

MAKES 12 servings   **PREP** 20 minutes   **BAKE** 16 minutes at 400°F

2½   **cups all-purpose flour**
2   **tablespoons sugar**
1   **tablespoon baking powder**
¼   **teaspoon salt**
½   **cup butter, cut into chunks (1 stick)**
¾   **cup chopped fresh strawberries**
½   **cup freeze-dried strawberries (optional)**
2   **tablespoons snipped basil**
2   **eggs, lightly beaten**
½   **cup half-and-half**
      Half-and-half or milk
      Sugar

1 Preheat oven to 400°F. In a large bowl stir together flour, the 2 tablespoons sugar, baking powder, and salt. Using a pastry blender or two knives, cut in butter until mixture resembles coarse crumbs. Gently toss in fresh and freeze-dried strawberries and, if using, basil. Make a well in center of flour mixture; set aside.

2 In a medium bowl stir together eggs and half-and-half. Add egg mixture to flour mixture all at once. Using a large spoon, gently stir just until moistened.

3 Turn dough out onto a generously floured surface. Knead dough by folding and gently pressing it five to seven times, turning dough a quarter turn after each fold. Transfer to a lightly floured parchment-lined baking sheet. Pat or lightly roll dough into a ¾-inch-thick circle. Cut circle into wedges and pull apart slightly.

4 Brush wedges with additional half-and-half and sprinkle with sugar. Bake for 16 minutes or until golden. Serve warm.

PER SERVING 209 **CAL**; 10 g **FAT** (6 g **SAT**); 60 mg **CHOL**; 211 mg **SODIUM**; 26 g **CARB**; 1 g **FIBER**; 4 g **PRO**

Vanilla French Toast

Using dry bread in this vanilla-scented French toast helps the slices stay firm without getting soggy when dipped in the egg mixture.

MAKES 4 servings **PREP** 10 minutes **COOK** 4 minutes

4	**eggs, lightly beaten**
1	**cup half-and-half or light cream**
2	**tablespoons sugar**
2	**teaspoons vanilla**
1	**teaspoon ground cinnamon**
¼	**teaspoon ground nutmeg**
8	**slices dry white or whole wheat bread**
2	**tablespoons butter or vegetable oil**
	Maple-flavor syrup
	Sliced bananas (optional)

1 In a shallow bowl beat together eggs, half-and-half, sugar, vanilla, cinnamon, and nutmeg. Dip bread slices into egg mixture, coating both sides.

2 In an extra-large skillet or on a griddle, melt 1 tablespoon of the butter over medium heat. Cook half the bread slices for 4 to 6 minutes or until golden, turning once. Repeat with remaining butter and the remaining bread slices. Serve with maple syrup and sliced bananas.

PER SERVING 472 **CAL**; 20 g **FAT** (10 g **SAT**); 249 mg **CHOL**; 421 mg **SODIUM**; 62 g **CARB**; 2 g **FIBER**; 14 g **PRO**

Pumpkin Waffles with Maple-Walnut Cream

A decadent melange of maple syrup, butter, walnuts, and whipping cream tops off these waffles.
Although pure maple syrup is a bit pricey, the flavor is worth the splurge.

MAKES 12 servings **START TO FINISH** 35 minutes

- 4   cups all-purpose flour
- ¼   cup packed brown sugar
- 2   tablespoons baking powder
- 1   teaspoon salt
- 1   teaspoon ground cinnamon
- ½   teaspoon ground ginger
- ½   teaspoon ground nutmeg
- 4   eggs, lightly beaten
- 3   cups milk
- 1   15-ounce can pumpkin
- ¼   cup butter, melted
- 1   recipe Maple-Walnut Cream

1 In a large bowl stir together flour, brown sugar, baking powder, salt, cinnamon, ginger, and nutmeg. Make a well in the center of flour mixture.

2 In another large bowl combine eggs, milk, pumpkin, and melted butter. Add pumpkin mixture all at once to flour mixture. Stir just until moistened (batter should be slightly lumpy).

3 For each waffle, add batter to a preheated, lightly greased waffle baker according to manufacturer's directions. Bake according to manufacturer's directions. When done, use a fork to lift waffle off grid. Serve warm with Maple-Pecan Cream.

Maple-Walnut Cream In a medium saucepan melt 1 tablespoon butter over medium heat. Add ¾ cup coarsely chopped walnuts or pecans. Cook and stir for 1 to 2 minutes or until walnuts are toasted. Stir in 1½ cups pure maple syrup and ½ cup whipping cream; heat through. Makes 2½ cups.

PER SERVING 465 **CAL**; 17 g **FAT** (7 g **SAT**); 102 mg **CHOL**; 408 mg **SODIUM**; 70 g **CARB**; 3 g **FIBER**; 10 g **PRO**

Cranberry-Buttermilk Muffins

Bursts of tart fresh cranberry punctuate these tender, not-too-sweet muffins.

MAKES 12 servings **PREP** 20 minutes **BAKE** 15 minutes at 400°F

1	**cup fresh cranberries**
2	**tablespoons sugar**
2	**cups all-purpose flour**
⅓	**to ½ cup sugar**
4	**teaspoons baking powder**
1	**teaspoon finely shredded orange peel**
½	**teaspoon salt**
1	**egg, lightly beaten**
¾	**cup buttermilk***
¼	**cup butter, melted**
	Coarse sugar

1 Preheat oven to 400°F. Grease twelve 2½-inch muffin cups or line with paper bake cups. In a medium bowl toss cranberries with 2 tablespoons sugar; set aside.

2 In a large bowl combine flour, ⅓ to ½ cup sugar, the baking powder, orange peel, and salt; stir well. In a small bowl combine egg, buttermilk, and butter. Make a well in center of flour mixture; add egg mixture and cranberries. Stir just until moistened. Spoon batter into prepared muffin cups. Sprinkle tops with coarse sugar.

3 Bake muffins for 15 minutes or until golden and a toothpick inserted in centers comes out clean. Cool on a wire rack. Serve warm.

*Tip If you don't have buttermilk, substitute sour milk. To make sour milk place 1 tablespoon of lemon juice or vinegar in a 1 cup glass measuring cup. Add enough milk to make 1 cup total liquid; stir. Let the mixture stand for 5 minutes before measuring the amount of sour milk needed for the recipe.

PER SERVING 163 **CAL**; 5 g **FAT** (3 g **SAT**); 29 mg **CHOL**; 306 mg **SODIUM**; 27 g **CARB**; 1 g **FIBER**; 3 g **PRO**

COCONUT-PECAN
COFFEE CAKE

Coconut-Pecan Coffee Cake

The gooey German chocolate cakelike layer of cinnamon-scented chocolate, coconut, and pecans surrounds this rich sour cream coffee cake.

MAKES 12 servings **PREP** 30 minutes
BAKE 55 minutes at 325°F **COOL** 1 hour

½	**cup butter, softened**
1	**cup granulated sugar**
2	**teaspoons baking powder**
½	**teaspoon baking soda**
¼	**teaspoon salt**
2	**eggs**
1	**teaspoon vanilla**
2¼	**cups all-purpose flour**
1	**8-ounce carton sour cream**
1	**recipe Coconut-Pecan Topping**

1 Preheat oven to 325°F. Grease and flour a 10-inch fluted tube pan; set aside. In a large mixing bowl beat butter with an electric mixer on medium for 30 seconds. Add the sugar, baking powder, baking soda, and salt. Beat until well combined, scraping sides of bowl occasionally. Add eggs, one at a time, beating well after each addition. Beat in vanilla. Alternately add flour and sour cream, beating on low after each addition just until combined.

2 Sprinkle half the Coconut-Pecan Topping in the prepared pan. Spoon half the batter in mounds over the coconut mixture; carefully spread evenly. Sprinkle with remaining Coconut-Pecan Topping. Spoon on remaining batter, spreading evenly.

3 Bake for 55 to 65 minutes or until a wooden toothpick inserted near the center comes out clean. Cool in pan on a wire rack for 10 minutes. Remove cake from pan; cool completely on wire rack.

Coconut-Pecan Topping In a large bowl combine 1 cup all-purpose flour, 1 cup packed brown sugar, and 1 teaspoon ground cinnamon. Using a pastry blender, cut in ½ cup cold butter, cut up, until mixture resembles coarse crumbs. Stir in ¾ cup semisweet chocolate pieces, ½ cup flaked coconut, and ½ cup chopped pecans.

PER SERVING 550 **CAL**; 28 g **FAT** (16 g **SAT**); 86 mg **CHOL**; 297 mg **SODIUM**; 71 g **CARB**; 2 g **FIBER**; 6 g **PRO**

Dark Chocolate, Raisin, and Nut Granola

Wrap up 6-serving portions of this healthful granola in pretty cellophane bags labeled and tied with bows to give as gifts.

MAKES 18 servings **PREP** 25 minutes
BAKE 45 minutes at 325°F

½	**cup unsweetened applesauce**
¼	**cup packed brown sugar**
2	**tablespoons unsalted butter**
2	**tablespoons honey**
1	**tablespoon vanilla**
1	**teaspoon sea salt**
3	**cups rolled oats**
¾	**cup pistachio nuts**
¾	**cup slivered almonds**
½	**cup pumpkin seeds (pepitas)**
½	**cup raw sunflower kernels**
2	**tablespoons ground cinnamon**
1½	**cups raisins**
1	**cup dark chocolate pieces**

1 Preheat oven to 325°F. In a small saucepan combine applesauce, brown sugar, butter, honey, vanilla, and salt. Cook and stir over low heat until butter is melted and brown sugar is dissolved.

2 In an extra-large bowl combine oats, pistachio nuts, almonds, pumpkin seeds, sunflower kernels, and cinnamon. Drizzle applesauce mixture over oats mixture; stir to coat. Transfer to a 15 x 10 x 1-inch baking pan or a shallow roasting pan.

3 Bake for 45 minutes, stirring twice. Stir in raisins. Transfer to an extra-large bowl; cool. Stir in chocolate pieces. Store in an airtight container.

PER SERVING 273 **CAL**; 14 g **FAT** (4 g **SAT**); 4 mg **CHOL**; 93 mg **SODIUM**; 35 g **CARB**; 4 g **FIBER**; 7 g **PRO**

CHAPTER 3

meals in minutes

Eat deliciously and quickly with these recipes—to the table in 30 minutes.

BACON-WRAPPED SALMON
WITH FRUIT CHUTNEY

Korean Beef and Vegetable Bowls

Texan Teresa Cardin claims to know her beef—and the judges of the Region 4 National Beef Cook-Off agree. The homemaker, grandmother, and frequent recipe-contest competitor won first prize and $1,500 in the 2013 Semi-Homemade Beef Recipes category for this quick protein- and veggie-rich dish.

MAKES 4 servings **START TO FINISH** 25 minutes

1	cup uncooked long grain rice
1	beef flank steak (about 1 pound)
¼	teaspoon garlic salt
4	teaspoons toasted sesame oil
1	16-ounce package frozen broccoli stir-fry vegetable blend
1	cup bottled Korean barbecue sauce (such as Lee Kum Kee brand)

1 Prepare rice according to package directions. Set aside; keep warm.

2 Meanwhile, cut beef lengthwise in half then cut crosswise against the grain into thin bite-size strips. Sprinkle meat with garlic salt.

3 In a large nonstick skillet cook beef in 1 teaspoon of the sesame oil over medium-high heat until desired doneness. Remove from skillet; keep warm. Repeat with remaining beef and 1 teaspoon of the sesame oil. Remove from skillet.

4 In the same skillet heat remaining 2 teaspoons sesame oil over medium-high heat. Add broccoli stir-fry blend; cook and stir 4 minutes. Return beef to skillet; add rice and sauce. Cook for 1 to 2 minutes or until heated through and vegetables are crisp-tender. Serve in bowls.

PER SERVING 528 **CAL**; 13 g **FAT** (4 g **SAT**); 74 mg **CHOL**; 2,199 mg **SODIUM**; 67 g **CARB**; 3 g **FIBER**; 30 g **PRO**

Brown Sugar Pork Chops with Onions

Steamed fresh green beans make a nice accompaniment to these pan-seared chops topped with caramelized onions.

MAKES 4 servings **START TO FINISH** 25 minutes

- **2** teaspoons vegetable oil
- **4** boneless pork rib or loin chops, cut ½ to ¾ inch thick
- **¼** teaspoon black pepper
- **1** medium onion, halved lengthwise and thinly sliced
- **¼** cup orange juice
- **2** tablespoons packed brown sugar
- **¼** teaspoon crushed red pepper (optional)

1 In a large skillet heat oil over medium heat. Sprinkle chops with black pepper. Cook chops in hot oil for 6 to 8 minutes, until slightly pink in center, turning once. Remove chops from skillet; cover and keep warm.

2 For sauce, in the same skillet cook and stir onion over medium heat about 3 minutes or until tender. Push onion aside. Remove skillet from heat; add orange juice and brown sugar. Return to heat. Cook and stir for 1 minute or until sugar is dissolved. Stir onions into sauce.

3 Place a chop on each of 4 plates. Top with some of the sauce, and, if desired, sprinkle with crushed red pepper.

PER SERVING 304 **CAL**; 18 g **FAT** (6 g **SAT**); 68 mg **CHOL**; 51 mg **SODIUM**; 11 g **CARB**; 1 g **FIBER**; 23 g **PRO**

Bacon Tomato-Melts

Make these knife-and-fork open-faced sandwiches in summer, when the tomatoes are sweet, ripe, and juicy.

MAKES 4 servings **START TO FINISH** 25 minutes

- 2 **large tomatoes**
- ¼ **cup light sour cream**
- 1 **green onion, thinly sliced**
- 1 **clove garlic, minced**
- ⅛ **teaspoon cayenne pepper or ¼ teaspoon paprika**
- ⅛ **teaspoon ground cumin**
- 4 **½-inch slices bakery-style or sandwich-style whole wheat bread**
- 2 **cups fresh spinach leaves**
- 8 **slices turkey bacon, cooked according to package directions**
- ½ **cup shredded reduced-fat Mexican-style cheese blend (2 ounces)**

1 Preheat broiler. Slice tomatoes. Seed and chop 1 or 2 of the slices to equal ¼ cup chopped tomato. Set remaining tomato slices aside. For sauce, in a small bowl combine the ¼ cup chopped tomato, sour cream, green onion, garlic, cayenne pepper, and cumin. Set aside.

2 Place bread slices on a baking sheet. Broil 4 to 5 inches from the heat for 2 to 3 minutes or until toasted, turning once. Top bread slices with the spinach leaves, tomato slices, sour cream sauce, and bacon. Top with cheese. Broil for 1 to 2 minutes or until cheese is melted.

PER SERVING 206 **CAL**; 10 g **FAT** (5 g **SAT**); 42 mg **CHOL**; 623 mg **SODIUM**; 15 g **CARB**; 3 g **FIBER**; 12 g **PRO**

Roasted BLT Salad

This deconstructed BLT is a delicious combination of textures, tastes, and temperatures. Warm cherry tomatoes and slightly wilted romaine are tossed with crisp-cooked bacon and crunchy homemade croutons.

MAKES 4 servings **PREP** 10 minutes **BAKE** 15 minutes at 400°F **STAND** 5 minutes

4	slices bacon
1	cup cherry tomatoes
6	teaspoons olive oil
½	baguette, cut into 1½-inch cubes
1	head romaine lettuce, quartered lengthwise
¼	teaspoon salt
¼	teaspoon black pepper

1 Preheat oven to 400°F. In a large skillet cook bacon until crisp; drain on paper towels. Break into large pieces; set aside.

2 Meanwhile, line a 15 x 10 x 1-inch baking pan with foil. Add cherry tomatoes; toss with 2 teaspoons of the olive oil. Bake, uncovered, for 10 minutes. Transfer tomatoes and their juices to a medium bowl. Place bread cubes and romaine quarters on the baking pan. Drizzle romaine with 2 teaspoons of the olive oil. Return pan to oven; bake 5 minutes or until bread is golden and romaine is browned on edges.

3 Add bread to the medium bowl with the tomatoes. Toss gently to combine. Let stand 5 minutes to allow bread to absorb some of the tomato juices. Transfer tomatoes, bread, romaine, and bacon to a serving platter. Drizzle with the remaining 2 teaspoons olive oil. Season with salt and pepper.

PER SERVING 258 **CAL**; 10 g **FAT** (2 g **SAT**); 9 mg **CHOL**; 647 mg **SODIUM**; 31 g **CARB**; 2 g **FIBER**; 8 g **PRO**

Chicken and Pasta Frittata

This one-dish dinner is a clever way to use up leftover cooked pasta and chicken.

MAKES 4 servings **START TO FINISH** 30 minutes **OVEN** 5 minutes at 400°F

1	**cup broccoli florets**
½	**cup chopped onion (1 medium)**
2	**tablespoons olive oil**
1¼	**cups cooked penne or other pasta**
1	**cup chopped cooked chicken**
2	**tablespoons snipped fresh basil**
¼	**teaspoon salt**
¼	**teaspoon black pepper**
8	**eggs, lightly beaten**
½	**cup shredded mozzarella cheese (2 ounces)**
	Black pepper

1 Preheat oven to 400°F. In a large oven-going skillet cook broccoli and onion in hot oil over medium heat for 5 minutes or until tender, stirring occasionally. Stir in pasta, chicken, basil, salt, and the ¼ teaspoon pepper.

2 Pour eggs over mixture in skillet. Cook over medium heat, without stirring, until eggs begin to set on bottom and around edges. Using a spatula or large spoon, lift and fold the partially cooked eggs so the uncooked portion flows underneath. Continue cooking until eggs are nearly set. Sprinkle with cheese. Transfer to oven. Bake for 5 minutes or until set. Sprinkle with additional pepper.

PER SERVING 415 **CAL**; 23 g **FAT** (7 g **SAT**); 462 mg **CHOL**; 421 mg **SODIUM**; 23 g **CARB**; 2 g **FIBER**; 30 g **PRO**

Chicken-Broccoli Mac and Cheese

A package of semisoft cheese flavored with garlic and herbs provides creaminess and flavor for the super-quick sauce.

MAKES 4 servings **START TO FINISH** 25 minutes

8	ounces dried rigatoni
2	cups fresh broccoli florets
1	2- to 2¼-pound whole roasted chicken
1	5.2-ounce package semisoft cheese with garlic and fine herbs
¾	to 1 cup milk
¼	cup oil-packed dried tomatoes, drained and snipped
¼	teaspoon freshly ground black pepper
	Snipped fresh parsley (optional)

1 In a large saucepan cook pasta according to package directions, adding broccoli during the last 3 minutes of cooking. Meanwhile, remove chicken from bones; discard bones. Coarsely chop chicken. Drain pasta and broccoli; set aside.

2 In the same saucepan combine cheese, ¾ cup of the milk, the tomatoes, and pepper. Cook and stir until cheese is melted. Add pasta, broccoli, and chicken. Heat through. If necessary, thin with some of the remaining milk. If desired, sprinkle with parsley.

PER SERVING 667 **CAL**; 34 g **FAT** (15 g **SAT**); 163 mg **CHOL**; 872 mg **SODIUM**; 52 g **CARB**; 3 g **FIBER**; 40 g **PRO**

MEDITERRANEAN CHICKEN SALAD

Mediterranean Chicken Salad

Mediterranean favorites—garbanzo beans, kalamata olives, and feta cheese—give this healthful salad contrasting texture and flavor. Serve it with warmed pita bread.

MAKES 6 servings **START TO FINISH** 20 minutes

⅓	cup lemon juice
2	tablespoons snipped fresh mint
2	tablespoons snipped fresh basil
2	tablespoons olive oil
1	tablespoon honey
¼	teaspoon black pepper
5	cups shredded romaine lettuce
2	cups cut-up cooked chicken breast
2	plum tomatoes, cut into wedges
1	15-ounce can garbanzo beans (chickpeas), rinsed and drained
2	tablespoons pitted kalamata olives, quartered
2	tablespoons crumbled reduced-fat feta cheese
12	whole kalamata olives

1 For dressing, in a screw-top jar combine lemon juice, mint, basil, oil, honey, and pepper. Cover and shake well.

2 Place lettuce on a large platter. Top with chicken, tomatoes, beans, the quartered olives, and cheese. Drizzle with dressing. Garnish individual servings with whole olives.

PER SERVING 252 **CAL**; 9 g **FAT** (1 g **SAT**); 41 mg **CHOL**; 422 mg **SODIUM**; 24 g **CARB**; 5 g **FIBER**; 19 g **PRO**

Lemon-Ginger Chicken Thighs

The simplest way to grate fresh ginger is on a Microplane grater or zester. If you don't have one, think about getting one. They can be used for ginger, garlic, citrus peel, and whole nutmeg.

MAKES 4 servings **START TO FINISH** 30 minutes

1	lemon
1	tablespoon grated fresh ginger
½	teaspoon salt
2	tablespoons honey
2	tablespoons water
1	tablespoon reduced-sodium soy sauce
8	bone-in chicken thighs
2	teaspoons vegetable oil
	Sliced green onions (optional)
	Lemon wedges (optional)

1 Finely shred peel from lemon then juice lemon. In a small bowl combine lemon peel, ginger, and salt. In another small bowl combine lemon juice, honey, the water, and soy sauce.

2 Rub lemon peel mixture under the skin of chicken thighs. In an extra-very large skillet heat oil over medium-high heat. Cook chicken, skin sides down, in hot oil about 7 minutes or until well browned. Turn chicken; add lemon juice mixture. Reduce heat. Cook, covered, for 14 to 18 minutes or until done (180°F).

3 Transfer chicken to dinner plates. If desired, skim fat from pan juices and drizzle juices over chicken. If desired, sprinkle with green onions and serve with lemon wedges.

PER SERVING 459 **CAL**; 31 g **FAT** (8 g **SAT**); 158 mg **CHOL**; 567 mg **SODIUM**; 12 g **CARB**; 1 g **FIBER**; 33 g **PRO**

Turkey-Vegetable Casserole

These individual casseroles are a tasty dish that calls for leftover Thanksgiving turkey.

MAKES 4 servings **PREP** 15 minutes
BAKE 10 minutes at 450°F

1   16-ounce bag frozen stew vegetables (potatoes, carrots, onion, and celery)
1   18-ounce jar home-style gravy (1¾ cups)
1   teaspoon finely snipped fresh sage or ½ teaspoon ground sage
2   cups cut-up cooked turkey or chicken
1   medium cooking apple, thinly sliced
    Fresh sage leaves (optional)
2   tablespoons butter, melted
¼   teaspoon ground nutmeg
¼   teaspoon black pepper

1 Preheat oven to 450°F. In a large microwave-safe bowl combine vegetables, gravy, and the 1 teaspoon sage. Cover with vented plastic wrap. Heat on high for 5 minutes. Add turkey; cover and microwave for 4 to 6 minutes or until heated through and vegetables are tender, stirring occasionally.

2 Spoon turkey filling into four 14- to 16-ounce casseroles. Top with apple and, if desired, fresh sage leaves. Drizzle with melted butter. In a small bowl stir together nutmeg and pepper; sprinkle over casseroles.

3 Bake, uncovered, about 10 minutes or until bubbly and apple slices begin to brown.

PER SERVING 297 **CAL**; 12 g **FAT** (5 g **SAT**); 71 mg **CHOL**; 753 mg **SODIUM**; 23 g **CARB**; 3 g **FIBER**; 24 g **PRO**

Bacon-Wrapped Salmon with Fruit Chutney

The tartness of the cranberries combined with the sweetness of apricot jam and the smokiness of the bacon gives this super quick dish (21 minutes!) fabulous flavor.

MAKES 4 servings **START TO FINISH** 21 minutes

4   4-ounce fresh or frozen skinless salmon fillets, about ½ inch thick
8   slices center cut bacon
    Salt
    Black pepper
1   teaspoon olive oil
½   cup fresh or frozen cranberries, coarsely chopped
⅓   cup apricot jam
1   teaspoon fresh thyme leaves

1 Thaw fish, if frozen. Line a microwave-safe plate with paper towels. Place 4 slices of the bacon on the plate. Cook on high for 1½ minutes. Repeat with the remaining 4 slices bacon.

2 Rinse salmon; pat dry with paper towels. Lightly sprinkle with salt and pepper. Wrap 2 bacon slices around each fillet. In an extra large skillet heat olive oil over medium-high heat. Add salmon, bacon seam sides down; cook for 3 minutes. Turn salmon; cook for 3 to 5 minutes more or until bacon is crisp and salmon flakes when tested with a fork.

3 For chutney, in a small saucepan combine cranberries and jam. Cook over medium heat until heated through, stirring occasionally. Serve salmon with chutney. Top with thyme.

PER SERVING 341 **CAL**; 15 g **FAT** (4 g **SAT**); 80 mg **CHOL**; 706 mg **SODIUM**; 20 g **CARB**; 1 g **FIBER**; 28 g **PRO**

BACON-WRAPPED SALMON
WITH FRUIT CHUTNEY

GNOCCHI WITH
MUSHROOMS AND TUNA

Gnocchi with Mushrooms and Tuna

Dishes you can cook from your pantry (which includes your refrigerator and freezer) are especially helpful on the busiest nights. This dish brings together shelf-stable gnocchi and canned tuna with fresh mushrooms. Just a quick stop at the store and you're ready to cook!

MAKES 4 servings **PREP** 10 minutes
BAKE 12 minutes at 425°F **STAND** 5 minutes

1	16-ounce package shelf-stable potato gnocchi
4	cups assorted small and/or sliced fresh mushrooms, such as shiitake or cremini
2	cloves garlic, minced
1	tablespoon olive oil
1	cup half-and-half
2	5-ounce cans solid light tuna packed in oil, drained and broken into chunks
2	ounces Parmesan cheese, shaved Fresh basil leaves (optional)
¼	teaspoon crushed red pepper

1 Preheat oven to 425°F. Lightly grease a 1½-quart gratin dish; set aside. In a large saucepan cook gnocchi in lightly salted water according to package directions; drain.

2 Meanwhile, in a large skillet cook mushrooms and garlic in hot oil over medium heat until tender. Stir in half-and-half. Simmer, uncovered, for 5 to 7 minutes or until liquid begins to thicken. Fold in gnocchi and tuna. Transfer to the prepared dish.

3 Bake, uncovered, for 12 to 15 minutes or until lightly browned. Sprinkle with Parmesan cheese. Let stand for 5 minutes. Top with basil leaves, if desired, and crushed red pepper.

PER SERVING 521 **CAL**; 21 g **FAT** (9 g **SAT**); 45 mg **CHOL**; 920 mg **SODIUM**; 48 g **CARB**; 4 g **FIBER**; 35 g **PRO**

Pizza Primavera

"Primavera" may mean "spring" in Italian, but culinarily speaking, it means an abundance of fresh vegetables. These individual pizzas made with whole-wheat flatbreads are topped with asparagus, sweet peppers, red onion, mushrooms, and cherry tomatoes.

MAKES 4 servings **PREP** 15 minutes
ROAST 15 minutes at 475°F

2	cups cut-up fresh asparagus
2	yellow sweet peppers, cut into thin bite-size strips
2	medium red onions, sliced
8	fresh mushrooms, sliced
4	teaspoons olive oil
½	teaspoon salt
4	whole wheat flatbreads
½	cup grated Pecorino-Romano cheese (2 ounces)
2	cups halved cherry tomatoes
½	cup shredded mozzarella cheese (2 ounces)

1 Preheat oven to 475°F. Line a large baking sheet with parchment paper; set aside. In a large bowl combine asparagus, sweet peppers, onions, mushrooms, oil, and salt. Spoon vegetable mixture onto prepared baking sheet, spreading in an even layer. Roast for 10 minutes; remove from oven and set aside.

2 Place flatbreads on two large baking sheets; sprinkle Pecorino-Romano cheese evenly over flatbreads. Evenly arrange the roasted vegetables and the cherry tomatoes on flatbreads. Sprinkle with mozzarella cheese. Bake for 5 minutes or until cheese is melted.

PER SERVING 329 **CAL**; 14 g **FAT** (5 g **SAT**); 22 mg **CHOL**; 875 mg **SODIUM**; 39 g **CARB**; 11 g **FIBER**; 20 g **PRO**

Beans and Greens with Corn Bread Croutons

The corn bread croutons will be crisper if they're made with day-old corn bread, so try to buy or make the corn bread a day ahead, if you can. If not, they will get toasty enough in the oven.

MAKES 4 servings **PREP** 15 minutes **BAKE** 10 minutes at 400°F

12 **ounces purchased or homemade corn bread**
    Nonstick cooking spray
2   **tablespoons finely shredded Parmesan cheese**
3   **tablespoons olive oil**
1   **red onion, thinly sliced**
3   **tablespoons red wine vinegar or balsamic vinegar**
1   **15-ounce can no-salt-added cannellini beans (white kidney beans), rinsed and drained**
2   **1-pound packages collard greens (torn), curly endive (torn), or baby spinach**
¼   **teaspoon salt**
½   **teaspoon black pepper**
    Finely shredded Parmesan cheese (optional)
    Crushed red pepper (optional)

1 Preheat oven to 400°F. For croutons, cut corn bread into 1-inch cubes (should have about 4½ cups). Place cubes in a 15 x 10 x 1-inch baking pan; lightly coat with cooking spray. Bake about 10 minutes or until crisp and golden. Remove from oven; sprinkle with the 2 tablespoons Parmesan cheese.

2 In an extra-large skillet heat 1 tablespoon of the oil over medium heat. Add onion; cook for 4 to 5 minutes or until tender. Stir in 2 tablespoons of the vinegar. Add beans; heat through. Transfer to a bowl; cover to keep warm.

3 Add the remaining 2 tablespoons oil to skillet. Add greens; cook and stir, in batches if necessary, just until wilted. Sprinkle with salt and black pepper; drizzle with the remaining 1 tablespoon vinegar.

4 To serve, top greens with beans and croutons. If desired, top with additional Parmesan cheese and sprinkle with crushed red pepper.

PER SERVING 490 **CAL**; 19 g **FAT** (3 g **SAT**); 36 mg **CHOL**; 827 mg **SODIUM**; 67 g **CARB**; 15 g **FIBER**; 17 g **PRO**

Asian-Style Fried Rice and Beans

Cold rice is best for making fried rice because the grains separate more easily than when it is hot. Cook brown rice ahead of time, cool completely, and fluff it to keep it from clumping. Keep cooked and cooled rice in a tightly sealed container in the refrigerator for up to 5 days.

MAKES 4 servings **START TO FINISH** 30 minutes

½ **fresh pineapple, peeled, cored, and sliced, or one 8-ounce can pineapple slices (juice pack)**

1 **tablespoon vegetable oil**

2 **medium carrots, very thinly sliced on the diagonal**

4 **cloves garlic, minced**

2 **teaspoons grated fresh ginger***

2 **cups cooked brown rice**

1 **15-ounce can garbanzo beans (chickpeas), rinsed and drained**

1 **cup frozen peas, thawed**

3 **tablespoons reduced-sodium soy sauce**

⅓ **cup snipped fresh cilantro**

1 **lime, halved**

Fresh cilantro leaves (optional)

1 Quarter the pineapple slices. In an extra-large nonstick skillet heat 2 teaspoons of the oil over medium heat. Add pineapple; cook for 4 minutes or until golden brown, turning once halfway through cooking time. Remove from skillet; set aside.

2 Reduce heat to medium. Add the remaining 1 teaspoon oil to the hot skillet. Add carrots; cook and stir for 5 minutes or just until tender. Add garlic and ginger; cook for 30 seconds.

3 Stir in brown rice, garbanzo beans, and peas. Stir in soy sauce. Cook and stir for 4 minutes or until heated through. Stir in the ⅓ cup cilantro. Return pineapple to pan.

4 To serve, squeeze lime over all. If desired, sprinkle with additional cilantro.

***Tip** Fresh ginger freezes beautifully. Place unpeeled ginger in a freezer bag. When a recipe calls for fresh, peel and grate in its frozen state, no thawing required.

PER SERVING 350 **CAL**; 6 g **FAT** (1 g **SAT**); 0 mg **CHOL**; 711 mg **SODIUM**; 65 g **CARB**; 10 g **FIBER**; 11 g **PRO**

Greek Spinach-Pasta Salad with Feta and Beans

Combine the beans, cheese, vegetables, and vinaigrette and let stand for up 2 hours before adding the cooked pasta. Any amount of standing time is good—it wilts the spinach a bit so it's easier to incorporate with the remaining ingredients.

MAKES 6 servings **PREP** 25 minutes **STAND** 2 hours

1   **5- to 6-ounce package fresh baby spinach**
1   **15-ounce can Great Northern beans, rinsed and drained**
1   **cup crumbled feta cheese (4 ounces)**
¼   **cup dried tomatoes (not oil-packed), snipped**
¼   **cup chopped green onions (2)**
2   **cloves garlic, minced**
1   **teaspoon finely shredded lemon peel**
2   **tablespoons lemon juice**
2   **tablespoons extra virgin olive oil**
1   **tablespoon snipped fresh oregano**
1   **tablespoon snipped fresh lemon thyme or thyme**
½   **teaspoon kosher salt or sea salt**
½   **teaspoon freshly ground black pepper**
12 **ounces dried cavatappi or farfalle pasta**
    Shaved Parmesan or Pecorino Romano cheese

1 In a large serving bowl combine spinach, beans, feta cheese, tomatoes, green onions, garlic, lemon peel, lemon juice, oil, oregano, thyme, salt, and pepper. Cover; let stand at room temperature up to 2 hours; stirring occasionally.

2 Shortly before serving, cook pasta according to package directions. Drain, reserving ¼ cup of the cooking water. Toss cooked pasta and reserved pasta water with spinach salad mixture. Serve warm or at room temperature. Top with shaved Parmesan cheese.

PER SERVING 408 **CAL**; 10 g **FAT** (4 g **SAT**); 19 mg **CHOL**; 487 mg **SODIUM**; 62 g **CARB**; 6 g **FIBER**; 17 g **PRO**

Corn and Bean Fritters with Tomatoes

Corn, beans, and tomatoes go together beautifully—especially in this bright and sunny summer dish.

MAKES 4 servings **START TO FINISH** 30 minutes

4	ears of fresh sweet corn or 2 cups frozen whole kernel corn, thawed
1	pound Campari and/or grape tomatoes
1	tablespoon vinegar
1	teaspoon salt
¼	cup water
1	15½-ounce can butter beans, rinsed and drained
1	6-ounce package Southern-style corn bread mix
1	egg
1	teaspoon ground ancho chili or chili powder
½	cup water
	Olive oil
	Fresh parsley or cilantro leaves (optional)

1 If using fresh corn, cut kernels from cobs; set aside.

2 Meanwhile, for the tomato ragu, coarsely chop, halve and/or slice tomatoes; transfer to a small saucepan. Add vinegar, ½ teaspoon of the salt, and the ¼ cup water. Cook, covered, on medium-low, stirring occasionally.

3 In a large mixing bowl mash beans with a fork. Add corn kernels, cornbread mix, egg, ground chili, the remaining ½ teaspoon salt, and the ½ cup water. Stir to combine.

4 Heat a large griddle or skillet over medium heat. Add 1 teaspoon oil to skillet. Add batter in scant ½ cup portions, cooking 4 at a time for about 4 minutes per side. Repeat with another teaspoon of oil and remaining batter.

5 Serve corn cakes topped with tomato ragu and, if desired, parsley.

PER SERVING 384 **CAL**; 11 g **FAT** (2 g **SAT**); 75 mg **CHOL**; 1,574 mg **SODIUM**; 65 g **CARB**; 10 g **FIBER**; 14 g **PRO**

Pumpkin, Barley, and Sage Soup

With pumpkin, maple syrup, sage, and sausage, this hearty soup is perfect for a warm-up on a cold fall night.

MAKES 4 servings **START TO FINISH** 30 minutes

- 1 tablespoon vegetable oil
- 8 ounces cooked andouille or smoked sausage links, chopped
- ⅓ cup chopped onion (1 small)
- 4 cups water
- 1 cup quick-cooking barley
- 1 tablespoon snipped fresh sage or 1 teaspoon dried sage, crushed
- 1 teaspoon instant chicken bouillon granules
- 1 15-ounce can pumpkin
- 2 tablespoons maple syrup
- 1 tablespoon cider vinegar
  Salt
  Black pepper
  Fresh sage leaves (optional)

1 In a 4-quart Dutch oven heat oil over medium heat. Add sausage and onion; cook for 3 minutes, stirring frequently. Add the water, barley, dried sage (if using), and bouillon granules.

2 Bring to boiling; reduce heat. Simmer, covered, for 12 minutes, stirring occasionally. Stir in pumpkin, maple syrup, and vinegar; cook until heated through. Season to taste with salt and pepper.

3 If desired, garnish each serving with fresh sage leaves.

PER SERVING 439 CAL; 21 g FAT (6 g SAT); 35 mg CHOL; 832 mg SODIUM; 51 g CARB; 11 g FIBER; 14 g PRO

Smoky Cheese and Potato Soup

Use any smoked cheese you like in this fabulously rich and creamy soup. For a vegetarian version, swap the ham for cannellini beans (see variation, below).

MAKES 4 servings **START TO FINISH** 25 minutes

- 1½ cups shredded smoked cheddar, smoked mozzarella, or smoked gouda cheese (6 ounces)
- 1 tablespoon all-purpose flour
- 1 cup finely chopped ham
- ½ cup finely chopped carrot (1 medium)
- ½ teaspoon curry powder
- ½ teaspoon paprika
- 3 cups whole milk
- ½ 24-ounce package refrigerated garlic mashed potatoes
  Canned shoestring potatoes, snipped fresh parsley and/or paprika (optional)

1 In a medium bowl combine cheese and flour; set aside.

2 In a Dutch oven combine the ham, carrot, curry powder, and paprika. Cook and stir over medium heat for 2 minutes. Stir in milk. Cook, uncovered, for 4 to 5 minutes or just until milk is hot but not boiling, stirring occasionally. Gradually whisk in mashed potatoes. Cook and stir until hot and bubbly. Stir in the cheese and flour. Cook and stir about 2 minutes or just until cheese is melted.

3 Ladle soup into bowls. If desired, top with shoestring potatoes, parsley, and/or paprika.

PER SERVING 429 CAL; 26 g FAT (16 g SAT); 94 mg CHOL; 1,059 mg SODIUM; 22 g CARB; 2 g FIBER; 25 g PRO

Cheese and Potato Soup with Beans Prepare as directed, except substitute 1 cup of cooked cannellini beans, rinsed and drained, for the ham and snipped fresh chives for the parsley.

SMOKY CHEESE AND POTATO SOUP

CHAPTER 4
cook it
slowly

At the end of a hectic day, sit down to a meal that's ready and waiting for you.

MEDITERRANEAN
MEAT LOAF

Mediterranean Meat Loaf

A hearty meat loaf dinner can be healthful. This flavorful version is made with lean ground beef, reduced-fat cheese, fat-free skim milk, and refrigerated egg product to ring in at just 238 calories and 9 grams of fat per serving.

MAKES 6 servings **PREP** 25 minutes
SLOW COOK 7 hours (low) or 3½ hours (high)

- ¼ **cup refrigerated or frozen egg product, thawed, or 1 egg, lightly beaten**
- 2 **tablespoons fat-free milk**
- ½ **cup fine dry bread crumbs**
- ½ **teaspoon dried oregano, crushed**
- ¼ **teaspoon black pepper**
- 2 **cloves garlic, minced**
- 1½ **pounds 95% lean ground beef**
- ½ **cup crumbled reduced-fat feta cheese (2 ounces)**
- ¼ **cup oil-packed dried tomatoes, drained and snipped**
- ¼ **cup bottled pizza or pasta sauce**
  Romaine leaves, matchstick carrots, and cucumber slices (optional)
  Red wine vinaigrette (optional)

1 In a large bowl combine egg product and milk; beat with a fork. Stir in bread crumbs, oregano, pepper, and garlic. Add ground beef, feta cheese, and dried tomatoes; mix well. Shape meat mixture into a 6-inch round loaf.

2 Cut an 18-inch-square sheet of heavy foil into thirds. Fold each piece into thirds lengthwise. Crisscross strips and place meat loaf in center of foil strips. Bringing up strips, transfer loaf and foil to a 3½- or 4-quart slow cooker (leave foil strips under loaf). Press loaf away from side of cooker. Fold strips down, exposing loaf. Spread pizza sauce over loaf.

3 Cover and cook on low-heat setting for 7 to 8 hours or on high-heat setting for 3½ to 4 hours.

4 Using foil strips, carefully lift meat loaf from cooker. Discard foil strips. If desired, combine romaine, carrots, and cucumbers; top with vinaigrette. Serve salad with meat loaf.

PER SERVING 238 **CAL**; 9 g **FAT** (4 g **SAT**); 74 mg **CHOL**; 324 mg **SODIUM**; 10 g **CARB**; 1 g **FIBER**; 29 g **PRO**

Brisket Ciabatta Sandwiches

Brisket is sold in two cuts: flat cut is the leanest and thinnest part of the brisket. Point cut is the thickest part of the brisket and is fattier and more tender, but you can use either cut in this recipe. Slow cooking makes either one meltingly tender.

MAKES 12 servings **PREP** 30 minutes **SLOW COOK** 9 hours (low) or 4½ hours (high)

- 1 **3-pound fresh beef brisket**
- 1 **cup sliced fresh cremini or button mushrooms**
- ½ **cup chopped onion (1 medium)**
- 2 **cloves garlic, minced**
- 1 **14.5-ounce can fire-roasted crushed or diced tomatoes, undrained**
- ½ **6-ounce can (⅓ cup) tomato paste with Italian seasonings or plain tomato paste**
- ¼ **cup dry red wine or beef broth**
- 1½ **teaspoons Worcestershire sauce**
- 1 **teaspoon dried Italian seasoning, crushed**
- ½ **teaspoon salt**
- ¼ **teaspoon ground black pepper**
- 12 **ciabatta buns, split and, if desired, toasted**
  Shredded Italian cheese blend (optional)

1 Trim fat from meat. If necessary, cut meat to fit into a 4- to 5-quart slow cooker. In the cooker combine mushrooms, onion, and garlic. Top with meat.

2 For sauce, in a medium bowl combine tomatoes, tomato paste, wine, Worcestershire sauce, Italian seasoning, salt, and pepper. Pour sauce over meat.

3 Cover and cook on low-heat setting for 9 to 10 hours or on high-heat setting for 4½ to 5 hours or until meat is tender. Transfer meat to a cutting board; cover with foil and keep warm. Skim fat from sauce.

4 If sauce is thin, transfer to a medium saucepan. Bring to boiling; reduce heat. Boil gently, uncovered, for 5 to 10 minutes or until slightly thickened.

5 Coarsely chop meat. Divide meat among bottoms of buns. Stir sauce into meat. If desired, top with cheese. Replace tops of buns. Pass any remaining sauce.

PER SERVING 596 **CAL**; 26 g **FAT** (10 g **SAT**); 81 mg **CHOL**; 809 mg **SODIUM**; 60 g **CARB**; 3 g **FIBER**; 30 g **PRO**

BRISKET CIABATTA SANDWICHES

Chili-Orange Short Ribs

Meaty short ribs are ideal candidates for a slow cooker. A long cooking time in flavorful liquid (in this case, sherry, orange juice, and soy sauce) makes the meat fall off the bones.

MAKES 6 servings **PREP** 20 minutes **SLOW COOK** 11 hours (low) or 5½ hours (high)

- 4- **to 5-pounds beef short ribs**
- 1½ **teaspoons kosher salt**
- ½ **teaspoon freshly ground black pepper**
- 3 **medium leeks, trimmed and cut into 2-inch lengths**
- 6 **cloves garlic, sliced**
- 1 **1-inch piece fresh ginger, peeled and sliced**
- 1 **star anise, broken**
- 1 **dried chile de arbol pepper**
- ½ **cup dry sherry or beef broth**
- 4 **2-inch strips orange peel**
- ½ **cup orange juice**
- ¼ **cup reduced-sodium soy sauce**
- 2 **tablespoons packed brown sugar**
- 3 **tablespoons chopped fresh cilantro**
  Clementines or tangerines, peeled and sectioned

1 Place ribs on a broiler pan. Sprinkle with salt and pepper. Broil 4 to 5 inches from the heat for 10 minutes or until browned.

2 Place leeks in a 5- to 6-quart slow cooker. Place ribs on leeks. Add garlic, ginger, star anise, and dried chile pepper. In a medium bowl combine sherry, orange peel, orange juice, soy sauce, and brown sugar. Pour over ribs in cooker. Cover; cook on low-heat setting for 11 to 12 hours or on high-heat setting for 5½ to 6 hours.

3 Using a slotted spoon or sieve, transfer ribs to a platter; cover to keep warm. Strain cooking liquid; discard solids. Skim fat from cooking liquid. Sprinkle ribs with cilantro. Serve cooking liquid with ribs for dipping. Serve ribs with clementines.

PER SERVING 834 **CAL**; 66 g **FAT** (28 g **SAT**); 152 mg **CHOL**; 986 mg **SODIUM**; 20 g **CARB**; 2 g **FIBER**; 34 g **PRO**

Creole Beef Stew

Onions, sweet pepper, and celery are referred to as the "holy trinity" of Cajun and Creole cooking —and they are all present in this Big-Easy-inspired stew.

MAKES 6 servings **PREP** 20 minutes **SLOW COOK** 8 hours (low) or 4 hours (high)

- 1 **cup chopped onion (1 large)**
- 1 **cup chopped green sweet pepper (1 large)**
- 1 **cup sliced celery (2 stalks)**
- 1 **cup fresh or frozen sliced okra**
- 2 **bay leaves**
- 1½ **pounds cubed lean beef stew meat***
- ¼ **teaspoon black pepper**
- 1 **14.5-ounce can diced tomatoes, undrained**
- 1 **cup reduced-sodium chicken broth**
- 3 **tablespoons tomato paste**
- 2 **tablespoons quick-cooking tapioca, crushed**
- 1 **teaspoon dried thyme leaf, crushed**
- ½ **teaspoon sugar**
- ½ **teaspoon salt**
- ¼ **to ½ teaspoon cayenne pepper**
- 1 **10-ounce bag frozen whole grain brown rice**
- 3 **tablespoons chopped fresh parsley (optional)**

1 Place onions, green sweet pepper, celery, okra, and bay leaves in a 4- to 5-quart slow cooker. Top with beef cubes; sprinkle with pepper. Combine undrained tomatoes, chicken broth, tomato paste, tapioca, thyme, sugar, salt, and cayenne pepper; pour over meat. Cover and cook on low-heat setting for 8 to 10 hours or on high-heat setting for 4 to 5 hours. Remove bay leaves.

2 Five minutes before serving, heat frozen brown rice according to package directions. Ladle stew into bowls over mounds of rice. If desired, garnish with chopped parsley.

***Tip** If you cannot locate lean stew meat, buy a 2½- to 2¾-pound boneless beef chuck roast. Trim fat off and cut into ¾-inch cubes.

PER SERVING 289 CAL; 7 g FAT (2 g SAT); 73 mg CHOL; 576 mg SODIUM; 27 g CARB; 3 g FIBER; 29 g PRO

Pulled Pork a la Maggie

Margaret Bracher looks for on-trend ingredients to use in the recipes she enters in cooking contests. Pomegranate molasses was a natural in this recipe that won her first place in the Pulled and Barbecue Pork category of the 2011 America's Next Pork Crock-Stars contest sponsored by the National Pork Board. Flavored with cumin, cinnamon, and fresh herbs and garlic, the meltingly tender meat won her $2,000 and a six-month supply of pork.

MAKES 8 servings **PREP** 20 minutes **SLOW COOK** 2 hours (high) + 5½ hours (low)

4	pounds boneless pork shoulder
2	teaspoons ground cumin
¾	teaspoon ground cinnamon
	Salt and black pepper
2	cups water
⅓	cup white vinegar
⅓	cup chopped onion (1 small)
1	tablespoon minced garlic
¼	cup pomegranate molasses
1	tablespoon olive oil
¼	cup finely chopped fresh parsley
¼	cup finely chopped fresh cilantro
8	slices Texas toast, toasted; or hamburger buns, split and toasted

1 Trim fat from meat; place in a 3½- or 4-quart slow cooker. Sprinkle with cumin, cinnamon, and salt and pepper to taste. Add the water, vinegar, onion, and garlic.

2 Cover and cook on high-heat setting for 2 hours. Reduce heat to low-heat setting and cook about 5 hours or until meat is very tender and falling apart.

3 Remove meat from cooker and discard cooking juices. Return meat to cooker and break apart with a fork or tongs. Stir in molasses and oil. Cover and cook for 30 minutes. Stir in the parsley and cilantro.

4 To serve, place pulled pork on Texas toast or buns.

PER SERVING 383 **CAL**; 11 g **FAT** (3 g **SAT**); 92 mg **CHOL**; 450 mg **SODIUM**; 36 g **CARB**; 1 g **FIBER**; 32 g **PRO**

Cuban Sandwiches with Dilled Cucumbers

A classic Cuban sandwich is made with roast pork, ham, Swiss cheese, pickles, and yellow mustard. This version swaps the cheese and pickles for a fresh and crunchy topping of Dilled Cucumbers.

MAKES 6 servings **PREP** 30 minutes **SLOW COOK** 8 hours (low) or 4 hours (high) + 30 minutes (high)

1	teaspoon dry mustard
½	teaspoon ground cumin
½	teaspoon black pepper
1	2½- to 3-pound pork sirloin roast
½	cup water
1	recipe Dilled Cucumbers
3	medium orange, yellow, and/or red sweet peppers, thinly sliced crosswise
2	medium banana peppers, stemmed, seeded, and thinly sliced crosswise
2	tablespoons yellow mustard
6	whole grain ciabatta buns, split and toasted
4	ounces thinly sliced cooked lower-sodium ham

1 In a small bowl combine dry mustard, cumin, and black pepper. Trim fat from roast. If necessary, cut roast to fit in a 3½- or 4-quart slow cooker. Sprinkle roast evenly with dry mustard mixture. Place roast in cooker; add the water.

2 Cover and cook on low-heat setting for 8 to 9 hours or on high-heat setting for 4 to 4½ hours. Meanwhile, prepare Dilled Cucumbers. If using low-heat setting, turn to high-heat setting. Add sweet peppers and banana peppers to slow cooker. Cover and cook for 30 minutes more.

3 Remove pork from cooker. Using two forks, coarsely shred pork; return pork to the cooking liquid.

4 Spread yellow mustard on split sides of ciabatta buns. Using a slotted spoon, divide pork among bun halves. Place ham over pork. Using a slotted spoon, remove peppers from cooker and spoon over ham. Using a slotted spoon, spoon Dilled Cucumbers onto sandwiches. If desired, drizzle some of the cucumber liquid over the sandwiches.

Dilled Cucumbers In a large bowl whisk together ½ cup cider vinegar, ¼ cup light mayonnaise, 4 teaspoons snipped fresh dill or 1 teaspoon dried dill, and ¼ teaspoon salt. Thinly slice 2 large English cucumbers; add to mayonnaise mixture with ¼ cup red onion slivers. Toss to coat. Cover and chill for 2 to 4 hours before serving. Makes about 4 cups.

PER SERVING 294 **CAL**; 8 g **FAT** (2 g **SAT**); 72 mg **CHOL**; 498 mg **SODIUM**; 25 g **CARB**; 3 g **FIBER**; 28 g **PRO**

Fire-Roasted Tomato and Italian Sausage Grinder

The filling for this family-pleasing sandwich goes into the slow cooker in less than 5 minutes. After simmering for hours, the rolls are stuffed and the sandwiches take a quick trip under the broiler to make the cheese melted and bubbly—yum!

MAKES 10 servings **PREP** 25 minutes **SLOW COOK** 6 hours (low) or 3 hours (high) **BROIL** 2 minutes

10 uncooked hot or sweet Italian sausage links (about 2½ pounds total)

2 14.5-ounce cans fire-roasted diced tomatoes, undrained

1 28-ounce can crushed tomatoes

1 tablespoon balsamic vinegar

6 cloves garlic, minced

2 teaspoons dried basil, crushed

1 teaspoon dried oregano, crushed

½ teaspoon salt

½ teaspoon crushed red pepper

¼ teaspoon black pepper

10 French-style rolls or hoagie buns, split

10 slices provolone cheese, halved

¾ cup roasted red sweet peppers, drained and cut into thin strips

1 Place sausage links in a 5- to 6-quart slow cooker. For sauce, stir in diced tomatoes, crushed tomatoes, vinegar, garlic, basil, oregano, salt, crushed red pepper, and black pepper.

2 Cover and cook on low-heat setting for 6 to 8 hours or on high-heat setting for 3 to 4 hours.

3 Preheat broiler. Place the sausage links on roll bottoms, reserving sauce in cooker. Place a half-slice of cheese on each sausage link and a half-slice of cheese on the cut side of each roll top. Place roll bottoms with sausage on a baking sheet. Broil 4 to 5 inches from the heat for 2 to 3 minutes or until cheese is melted and bubbly. Add roasted peppers and roll tops. Serve reserved sauce in individual serving bowls for dipping.

PER SERVING 859 **CAL**; 39 g **FAT** (17 g **SAT**); 96 mg **CHOL**; 2,305 mg **SODIUM**; 81 g **CARB**; 6 g **FIBER**; 37 g **PRO**

Apricot-Ginger Pork Chops

Most dried apricots are treated with sulfur dioxide to preserve their orange color—but some people have sensitivities to this preservative. If you're one of those people, look for unsulfured apricots at a natural-food store.

MAKES 6 servings **PREP** 25 minutes **SLOW COOK** 5 hours (low) or 2½ hours (high)

1	**16-ounce package frozen stir-fry vegetables**
6	**pork loin chops, cut ¾ inch thick**
2	**tablespoons vegetable oil**
¼	**teaspoon salt**
½	**cup apricot preserves**
½	**cup snipped dried apricots**
⅓	**cup plum sauce or sweet-and-sour sauce**
1	**tablespoon quick-cooking tapioca**
1½	**teaspoons grated fresh ginger or ½ teaspoon ground ginger**
2	**cloves garlic, minced**
2	**cups hot cooked basmati rice or long grain rice**
	Sliced green onions (optional)

1 Place frozen vegetables in a 4- to 5-quart slow cooker; set aside. Trim fat from chops. In a 12-inch skillet cook chops, half at a time, in hot oil over medium-high heat until browned on both sides. Drain off fat. Transfer chops to the cooker. Sprinkle with salt.

2. For sauce, in a small bowl combine apricot preserves, dried apricots, plum sauce, tapioca, ginger, and garlic. Pour sauce over chops.

3 Cover and cook on low-heat setting for 5 hours or on high-heat setting for 2½ hours.

4 Transfer chops and vegetables to a serving platter. Spoon some of the sauce over chops. Serve with rice and, if desired, sprinkle with green onions. Pass the remaining sauce.

PER SERVING 525 **CAL**; 20 g **FAT** (4 g **SAT**); 80 mg **CHOL**; 301 mg **SODIUM**; 54 g **CARB**; 3 g **FIBER**; 31 g **PRO**

Pork Ribs and Beans

Boneless pork country-style ribs, meaty and inexpensive, are often slow-cooked in barbecue sauce. This preparation has them mingling with Italian ingredients—herbs, beans, tomatoes, red wine, and Parmesan cheese.

MAKES 6 servings **PREP** 20 minutes **SLOW COOK** 8 hours (low) or 4 hours (high)

2	pounds boneless pork country-style ribs
1	teaspoon Italian seasoning, crushed
¾	teaspoon dried rosemary, crushed
¼	teaspoon ground black pepper
½	cup chopped onion (1 medium)
1	15- to 19-ounce can white kidney (cannellini) beans, rinsed and drained
1	15-ounce can black beans, rinsed and drained
1	14.5-ounce can no-salt-added diced tomatoes, undrained
¼	cup dry red wine or water
3	tablespoons shredded Parmesan cheese (optional)

1 Trim fat from meat. Sprinkle ribs with Italian seasoning, rosemary, and pepper. Place meat in a 3½- or 4-quart slow cooker. Place onion, beans, and tomatoes on meat; pour wine over all in cooker.

2 Cover and cook on low-heat setting for 8 to 9 hours or on high-heat setting for 4 to 4½ hours.

3 Using a slotted spoon, transfer meat and bean mixture to a serving bowl. Spoon some of the cooking liquid over meat and beans. If desired, sprinkle each serving with Parmesan cheese.

PER SERVING 325 **CAL**; 8 g **FAT** (3 g **SAT**); 111 mg **CHOL**; 415 mg **SODIUM**; 24 g **CARB**; 8 g **FIBER**; 41 g **PRO**

CHICKEN RAGOUT

Chicken Ragoût

A ragoût (ra-GOO) is a thick, well-seasoned stew that has its roots in French cooking.

MAKES 8 servings **PREP** 20 minutes
SLOW COOK 8 hours (low)

8	chicken thighs, skinned (about 3½ pounds)
2	14.5-ounce cans no-salt-added diced tomatoes, drained
3	cups 1-inch carrot slices or baby carrots
1	large onion, cut into wedges (1 cup)
⅓	cup reduced-sodium chicken broth
2	tablespoons white wine vinegar
1	teaspoon dried rosemary, crushed
1	teaspoon dried thyme, crushed
¼	teaspoon black pepper
8	ounces fresh button mushrooms, sliced
1	teaspoon olive oil
3	cups hot cooked whole wheat noodles
	Snipped fresh parsley (optional)

1 Place chicken thighs in a 3½- or 4-quart slow cooker. In a large bowl stir together tomatoes, carrots, onion, broth, vinegar, rosemary, thyme, and pepper. Pour over chicken.

2 Cover and cook on low-heat setting for 8 to 10 hours.

3 Just before serving, in a large nonstick skillet cook and stir mushrooms in hot oil over medium-high heat for 8 to 10 minutes or until golden. Remove chicken from cooker. Remove chicken from bones; discard bones. Stir chicken and mushrooms into ragoût in cooker. Serve chicken ragoût over hot cooked noodles. If desired, sprinkle each serving with parsley.

PER SERVING 234 **CAL**; 4 g **FAT** (1 g **SAT**); 57 mg **CHOL**; 163 mg **SODIUM**; 33 g **CARB**; 7 g **FIBER**; 20 g **PRO**

Hot and Spicy Braised Peanut Chicken

Jarred curry paste is a magical ingredient. Just a few teaspoons adds a world of flavor.

MAKES 6 servings **PREP** 30 minutes
SLOW COOK 5 hours (low) or 2½ hours (high)
STAND 5 minutes

2	onions, cut into thin wedges
1½	cups sliced carrots (3 medium)
1	red sweet pepper, cut into thin bite-size strips
2	pounds skinless, boneless chicken thighs, cut into 1-inch pieces
¾	cup chicken broth
3	tablespoons creamy peanut butter
½	teaspoon finely shredded lime peel
2	tablespoons lime juice
2	tablespoons soy sauce
2	tablespoons quick-cooking tapioca
1	tablespoon grated fresh ginger
2	to 3 teaspoons red curry paste
4	cloves garlic, minced
½	cup unsweetened coconut milk
1	cup frozen peas
	Hot cooked rice
	Chopped peanuts (optional)
	Snipped fresh cilantro (optional)

1 In a 3½- or 4-quart slow cooker place onions, carrots, and sweet pepper. Top with chicken. In a medium bowl whisk together broth, peanut butter, lime peel, lime juice, soy sauce, tapioca, ginger, curry paste, and garlic until smooth. Pour over chicken.

2 Cover and cook on low-heat setting for 5 to 6 hours or on high-heat setting for 2½ to 3 hours. Stir in coconut milk and peas. Let stand, covered, for 5 minutes.

3 Serve braised chicken over hot cooked rice. If desired, sprinkle individual servings with peanuts and cilantro.

PER SERVING 444 **CAL**; 15 g **FAT** (7 g **SAT**); 126 mg **CHOL**; 708 mg **SODIUM**; 39 g **CARB**; 4 g **FIBER**; 37 g **PRO**

Garam Masala Chicken Stew with Peas and Potatoes

Garam masala is an Indian spice blend that can vary in its ingredients, but it usually contains some combination of black pepper, cinnamon, cloves, coriander, cumin, cardamom, dried chiles, fennel, mace and/or nutmeg.

MAKES 6 servings **PREP** 20 minutes **SLOW COOK** 5½ hours (low) or 2¾ hours (high) + 15 minutes (high)

Nonstick cooking spray
- **6** large skinless, boneless chicken thighs (about 1½ pounds total)
- **2** medium red skinned potatoes, cut into ½-inch cubes (2 cups)
- **1** medium onion, thinly sliced
- **1½** teaspoons grated fresh ginger
- **2** cloves garlic, minced
- **½** teaspoon salt
- **½** teaspoon black pepper
- **1** 14.5-ounce can reduced-sodium chicken broth
- **1** 8-ounce can no-salt-added tomato sauce
- **1** cup frozen peas
- **½** cup plain fat-free yogurt
- **2** teaspoons garam masala

1 Lightly coat a large skillet with cooking spray; heat skillet over medium-high heat. Add chicken; cook about 6 minutes or until browned on both sides. Drain off fat.

2 In a 3½- or 4-quart slow cooker combine potatoes, onion, ginger, and garlic. Top with chicken. Sprinkle with salt and pepper. Pour broth and tomato sauce over vegetables and chicken.

3 Cover and cook on low-heat setting for 5½ hours or on high-heat setting for 2¾ hours.

4 If using low-heat setting, turn to high-heat setting. Stir in frozen peas, yogurt, and garam masala. Cover and cook for 15 minutes more.

PER SERVING 239 **CAL**; 5 g **FAT** (1 g **SAT**); 95 mg **CHOL**; 510 mg **SODIUM**; 20 g **CARB**; 4 g **FIBER**; 28 g **PRO**

Chicken Fajita Chili

This chili is so low fat (only 2 grams per serving!) you can top it with cheese, sour cream, and guacamole without an ounce of guilt.

MAKES 6 servings **PREP** 25 minutes **SLOW COOK** 4 hours (low) or 2 hours (high)

- 2 **pounds skinless, boneless chicken breast halves, cut into 1-inch pieces**
- 1 **tablespoon chili powder**
- 1 **teaspoon fajita seasoning**
- 2 **cloves garlic, minced**
- ½ **teaspoon ground cumin**
   Nonstick cooking spray
- 2 **14.5-ounce cans no-salt-added diced tomatoes, undrained**
- 1 **16-ounce package frozen yellow, green, and red peppers and onions**
- 1 **19-ounce can cannellini beans (white kidney beans), rinsed and drained**
- 3 **tablespoons shredded reduced-fat cheddar cheese (optional)**
- 3 **tablespoons light sour cream (optional)**
- 3 **tablespoons purchased guacamole (optional)**

1 In a medium bowl combine chicken, chili powder, fajita seasoning, garlic, and cumin; toss gently to coat. Set aside.

2. Coat a large skillet with cooking spray; heat skillet over medium-high heat. Cook half the chicken mixture at a time in hot skillet until browned, stirring occasionally. Transfer to a 3½- or 4-quart slow cooker. Stir tomatoes, frozen vegetables, and beans into chicken in slow cooker.

3 Cover and cook on low-heat setting for 4 to 5 hours or on high-heat setting for 2 to 2½ hours. If desired, top each serving with cheese, sour cream, and/or guacamole.

PER SERVING 261 **CAL;** 2 g **FAT** (1 g **SAT**); 88 mg **CHOL;** 294 mg **SODIUM;** 22 g **CARB;** 7 g FIBER; 41 g **PRO**

Pizza Stew with Biscuits

Kids will love this biscuit-topped stew flavored like one of their favorite foods.

MAKES 5 servings **PREP** 20 minutes **SLOW COOK** 3 hours (low) + 45 minutes (high)

8	ounces cremini mushrooms, quartered or sliced
¾	cup chopped green sweet pepper (1 medium)
⅓	cup finely chopped onion (1 small)
1	teaspoon dried Italian seasoning, crushed
¼	teaspoon salt
¼	teaspoon black pepper
2	cups marinara sauce
1¼	pounds uncooked ground turkey breast
¾	cup low-fat pancake and baking mix
⅓	cup grated Parmesan cheese
¼	teaspoon dried oregano, crushed
¼	cup fat-free milk
½	cup shredded part-skim mozzarella cheese (2 ounces) (optional)

1 In a 3½- to 4-quart slow cooker combine mushrooms, sweet pepper, onion, Italian seasoning, salt, and black pepper. Pour marinara sauce over all. Using a wooden spoon break up ground turkey into bite-size pieces. Add to cooker, stirring to combine.

2 Cover and cook on low-heat setting for 3 hours.

3 For biscuits, in a small bowl combine baking mix, Parmesan cheese, and oregano. Add milk; stir with a fork until combined.

4 Turn cooker to high-heat setting. Drop biscuit dough by tablespoons into 5 mounds onto hot stew, spacing mounds evenly.

5 Cover and cook for 45 to 60 minutes or until a toothpick inserted into biscuit centers comes out clean. If desired, sprinkle each serving with mozzarella cheese.

PER SERVING 323 **CAL**; 7 g **FAT** (2 g **SAT**); 62 mg **CHOL**; 851 mg **SODIUM**; 32 g **CARB**; 4 g **FIBER**; 33 g **PRO**

CHAPTER 5

great grilling

Fire up the grill and cook a mouthwatering meal for family and friends.

FLAT-IRON STEAKS CUBANO

BEEF

Blue Cheese-Stuffed Burgers with Red Onion
and Spinach, 92

Flat-Iron Steaks Cubano, 90

Hawaiian Burgers, 93

Santa Maria Strip Steaks with Red Sweet Peppers
and Onions, 90

PORK

Authentically Awesome Spare Ribs with
Fig-Jalapeño Sauce, 99

Cheese-Stuffed Knockwursts, 97

Grilled Pork and Noodle Salad, 96

Pork Tenderloin with Green Olive Tapenade, 95

Rhubarb-Glazed Pork Roast, 95

CHICKEN

Bricked Chicken with Grilled Oranges, 100

Cranberry-Chipotle Drumsticks, 101

FISH AND SEAFOOD

Spicy Grilled Shrimp, 102

Grilled Salmon and Asparagus with Garden
Mayonnaise, 102

MEATLESS

Grilled Vegetable Pizza, 104

Flat-Iron Steaks Cubano

Flat-iron steaks, a relatively new cut, are prized for tenderness and flavor relative to price.

MAKES 4 servings **PREP** 20 minutes
MARINATE 1 hour **GRILL** 7 minutes

4	beef shoulder top blade (flat-iron) steaks, cut ¾- to 1 inch thick (1½ pounds)
⅔	cup olive oil
2	to 3 tablespoons finely shredded orange peel*
½	cup orange juice*
⅓	cup finely chopped red onion (1 small)
1	tablespoon finely shredded lime peel*
¼	cup lime juice*
2	teaspoons finely shredded lemon peel*
3	tablespoons lemon juice*
6	cloves garlic, minced
2	teaspoons dried oregano, crushed
2	teaspoons ground cumin
1	teaspoon salt
½	teaspoon black pepper

1 Trim fat from steaks. Place steaks in a large resealable plastic bag set in a shallow dish. For marinade, in a medium bowl stir together oil, orange peel, orange juice, onion, lime peel, lime juice, lemon peel, lemon juice, garlic, oregano, cumin, salt, and pepper. Set aside ½ cup of the marinade until ready to serve.

2 Pour the remaining marinade over steaks in bag; seal bag. Turn to coat steaks. Marinate in the refrigerator for 1 to 2 hours, turning bag occasionally. Drain steaks, discarding marinade.

3 For a charcoal or gas grill, place steaks on a grill rack directly over medium heat. Cover and grill until 7 to 9 minutes for medium-rare (145°F) or 10 to 12 minutes for medium (160°F) desired doneness, turning once halfway through grilling.

4 Before serving, drizzle steaks with reserved marinade.

***Tip** To get enough citrus peel and juice for the marinade, use 2 oranges, 2 limes, and 1 lemon.

PER SERVING 374 **CAL**; 25 g **FAT** (6 g **SAT**); 102 mg **CHOL**; 296 mg **SODIUM**; 3 g **CARB**; 1 g **FIBER**; 33 g **PRO**

Santa Maria Strip Steaks with Red Sweet Peppers and Onions

A simple mixture of red wine vinegar, olive oil, and lots of fresh garlic acts as basting sauce for the meat and as dressing for the grilled peppers and onions.

MAKES 8 servings **PREP** 35 minutes **GRILL** 10 minutes

4	boneless beef top loin steaks (strip steaks), cut 1 inch thick (about 3 pounds total)
1	tablespoon kosher salt
1	tablespoon granulated garlic
1	teaspoon onion powder
1	teaspoon black pepper
1	teaspoon dried parsley flakes
2	medium red sweet peppers, stemmed, seeded, and quartered
2	medium red onions, cut into ½-inch slices
2	tablespoons olive oil
1	recipe Red Wine Vinegar Baste

1 Trim fat from steaks. For rub, in a small bowl combine the 1 tablespoon salt, the garlic, onion powder, black pepper, and parsley flakes. Generously sprinkle rub over all sides of steaks; rub in with your fingers. Brush sweet peppers and onions with oil. Sprinkle with additional salt.

2 For a charcoal or gas grill, place steaks on a grill rack directly over medium heat. Cover and grill 10 to 12 minutes for medium-rare (145°F) or 12 to 15 minutes for medium (160°F), turning once halfway through grilling and brushing frequently with half the Red Wine Vinegar. Add sweet peppers and onions to the grill for the last 10 minutes of grilling; turn once. Discard the Red Wine Vinegar Baste used during grilling.

3 Thinly slice sweet peppers and coarsely chop onions. Place vegetables in a large bowl. Drizzle with reserved Red Wine Vinegar Baste; toss to coat. Cut steaks in half crosswise and serve with vegetables.

Red Wine Vinegar Baste In a bowl whisk together ¼ cup red wine vinegar, ¼ cup olive oil, and 6 cloves garlic, minced.

PER SERVING 443 **CAL**; 30 g **FAT** (11 g **SAT**); 97 mg **CHOL**; 875 mg **SODIUM**; 6 g **CARB**; 1 g **FIBER**; 36 g **PRO**

SANTA MARIA STRIP STEAKS WITH
RED SWEET PEPPERS AND ONIONS

Blue Cheese-Stuffed Burgers with Red Onion and Spinach

Beef and blue cheese is a classic combination. Use any kind of blue cheese you like—American blue, Italian Gorgonzola, or French Roquefort.

MAKES 4 servings **PREP** 20 minutes **GRILL** 11 minutes

1	pound lean ground beef
1	tablespoon Worcestershire sauce
1	teaspoon freshly ground black pepper
⅓	to ½ cup crumbled blue cheese (about 2 ounces)
1	medium red onion, sliced crosswise
	Olive oil
	Salt
4	hamburger buns, split
1	cup fresh baby spinach

1 In a medium bowl combine ground beef, Worcestershire sauce, and pepper. On waxed paper, shape mixture into 8 thin 4-inch-diameter patties. Place 1 tablespoon of the cheese in the center of 4 patties. Top with the remaining 4 patties; pinch edges together to seal.

2 Brush onion slices with oil; sprinkle with salt.

3 For a charcoal or gas grill, place stuffed patties and onion slices on a grill rack directly over medium-high heat. Cover and grill for 10 to 14 minutes or thermometer registers 160°F, turning patties and onion slices once halfway through grilling. Meanwhile, brush cut sides of buns with oil. Add buns, cut sides down, to grill. Cover and grill about 1 minute or until toasted.

4 Serve patties in buns with onion slices, spinach, and the remaining cheese.

PER SERVING 497 **CAL**; 31 g **FAT** (12 g **SAT**); 89 mg **CHOL**; 638 mg **SODIUM**; 26 g **CARB**; 2 g **FIBER**; 27 g **PRO**

Hawaiian Burgers

Ham and crushed pineapple mixed into the meat gives these burgers tropical flair.
Tangy blue cheese offsets the sweetness of the fruit.

MAKES 8 servings **PREP** 20 minutes **GRILL** 14 minutes

2½	pounds lean ground beef
1	cup crumbled blue cheese (4 ounces)
1	cup finely chopped onion
1	8-ounce can crushed pineapple, drained
½	cup diced ham
1	2.8-ounce package cooked bacon pieces
2	teaspoons black pepper
1	teaspoon garlic powder
8	slices sharp cheddar cheese
8	hamburger buns or plain bagel thins
	Leaf lettuce (optional)
2	medium tomatoes, sliced (optional)
1	medium sweet onion, sliced (optional)

1 In an extra-large bowl combine beef, blue cheese, onion, pineapple, ham, bacon pieces, pepper, and garlic powder; mix well. Shape meat mixture into eight 1-inch-thick patties.

2 For a charcoal or gas grill, place patties on a grill rack directly over medium heat. Cover and grill for 12 to 14 minutes or thermometer registers 160°F, turning once halfway through grilling. Top patties with cheddar cheese. Grill, covered, for 2 minutes or until cheese is melted. Serve patties on buns. If desired, top with lettuce, tomatoes, and onion.

PER SERVING 596 **CAL**; 32 g **FAT** (15 g **SAT**); 137 mg **CHOL**; 951 mg **SODIUM**; 27 g **CARB**; 2 g **FIBER**; 46 g **PRO**

PORK TENDERLOIN WITH
GREEN OLIVE TAPENADE

Pork Tenderloin with Green Olive Tapenade

This elegant stuffed pork tenderloin is perfect for easy entertaining. Prepare the roll through Step 3 several hours ahead. Cover and refrigerate. Take it out of the refrigerator 30 minutes before grilling.

MAKES 6 servings **PREP** 40 minutes **GRILL** 35 minutes
STAND 10 minutes

1	cup pitted green olives
1	tablespoon drained capers
1	tablespoon Dijon mustard
1	tablespoon olive oil
1	tablespoon lemon juice
2	teaspoons anchovy paste
1	teaspoon snipped fresh thyme
1	clove garlic, minced
2	12- to 16-ounce pork tenderloins

1 For tapenade, in a food processor or blender, combine olives, capers, mustard, oil, lemon juice, anchovy paste, thyme, and garlic. Cover and process until nearly smooth, scraping down sides as necessary.

2 Trim fat from tenderloins. Make a lengthwise cut down the center of each tenderloin, cutting almost to, but not through, the opposite side. Spread meat open; place between plastic wrap. Using the flat side of a meat mallet lightly pound meat to make pliable. Overlap tenderloins about 2 inches along one long side. Lightly pound meat into a 12 x 10-inch rectangle. Remove plastic wrap.

3 Spread tapenade over meat to within 1 inch of the edges. Fold in long sides just to cover edge of tapenade. Starting at one of the short sides, roll up meat. To secure, tie at 1-inch intervals with 100%-cotton kitchen string.

4 For a charcoal grill, arrange medium-hot coals around a drip pan. Test for medium heat above pan. Place meat on grill rack over drip pan. Cover and grill for 35 to 40 minutes or until a thermometer registers 145°F. (For a gas grill, preheat grill. Reduce heat to medium. Adjust for indirect cooking. Grill as above, except place meat on a rack in a roasting pan; place pan on a grill rack.)

5 Remove meat from grill. Cover with foil; let stand for 10 minutes before slicing. Remove and discard strings.

PER SERVING 201 **CAL**; 10 g **FAT** (2 g **SAT**); 83 mg **CHOL**; 347 mg **SODIUM**; 1 g **CARB**; 27 g **PRO**

Rhubarb-Glazed Pork Roast

Rhubarb is prolific—if you have some in your yard, you need lots of good ways to use it. The pretty pink sauce for this grilled pork roast can be one of them.

MAKES 6 servings **PREP** 25 minutes **GRILL** 1 hour
STAND 15 minutes

2	cups fresh or frozen sliced rhubarb
1	6-ounce can frozen apple juice concentrate
	Several drops red food coloring (optional)
2	tablespoons honey
1	3- to 4-pound pork loin center rib roast, backbone loosened

1 For glaze, in a small saucepan combine rhubarb, apple juice concentrate, and, if desired, food coloring. Bring to boiling; reduce heat. Simmer, covered, for 15 to 20 minutes or until rhubarb is very tender. Press rhubarb glaze through a sieve into a small bowl, pressing out liquid with the back of a spoon; discard pulp. Return rhubarb glaze to saucepan. Return to boiling; reduce heat. Simmer, uncovered, about 5 minutes or until glaze is reduced to ½ cup. Remove from heat; stir in honey. Remove ¼ cup of the glaze to use for basting. Set aside remaining glaze until ready to serve.

2 Meanwhile, trim fat from meat. Insert a meat thermometer into the center of meat, making sure tip does not touch bone.

3 For a charcoal grill, arrange medium coals around a drip pan. Test for medium-low heat above pan. Place meat, bone side down, on a grill rack over drip pan. Cover and grill for 1 to 1½ hours or until a thermometer registers 145°F, brushing occasionally with the ¼ cup glaze during the last 15 minutes of grilling. (For a gas grill, preheat grill. Reduce heat to medium-low. Adjust for indirect cooking. Grill as above.) Discard glaze after basting.

4 Remove meat from grill. Cover with foil; let stand for 15 minutes before slicing. (Meat temperature will rise 10°F during standing.) Slice meat. Reheat and serve reserved glaze with meat.

PER SERVING 266 **CAL**; 7 g **FAT** (3 g **SAT**); 71 mg **CHOL**; 56 mg **SODIUM**; 19 g **CARB**; 29 g **PRO**

Grilled Pork and Noodle Salad

This Asian-style salad is a study in contrasts—cool and crunchy, then topped with slices of warm pork, just off the grill.

MAKES 4 servings **PREP** 25 minutes **MARINATE** 1 hour **GRILL** 5 minutes

3	boneless pork loin chops, cut ½ inch thick
½	cup bottled ginger vinaigrette salad dressing or balsamic vinaigrette salad dressing
¾	teaspoon anise seeds, crushed
1	7-ounce package rice sticks
⅓	cup vegetable oil
2	cups torn romaine lettuce
1½	cups thinly sliced peeled, seeded cucumber
½	cup coarsely snipped fresh mint leaves
½	cup coarsely snipped fresh Thai basil or basil leaves
½	cup shredded carrot (1 medium)
¼	cup coarsely chopped peanuts
	Thinly sliced cucumber
	Fresh cilantro sprigs
	Lime wedges (optional)

1 Trim fat from chops. Place chops in a resealable plastic bag set in a shallow dish. For marinade, in a small bowl combine ¼ cup of the ginger vinaigrette and ¼ teaspoon of the anise seeds. Pour marinade over chops in bag. Seal bag; turn to coat chops. Marinate in the refrigerator for 1 to 4 hours, turning bag occasionally.

2 Cook rice sticks according to package directions; drain in a colander. Rinse with cold water until water runs clear; drain for 20 minutes. Using kitchen scissors, snip rice sticks into 3- to 4-inch lengths. In a medium bowl combine rice sticks, oil, and the remaining ½ teaspoon anise seeds; toss gently to coat. Set aside.

3 Drain chops, discarding marinade. For a charcoal or gas grill, place chops on a grill rack directly over medium heat. Cover and grill for 4 to 5 minutes or until a thermometer registers 145°F, turning once halfway through grilling. Remove chops from grill and let stand 3 minutes. Slice diagonally.

4 In another medium bowl combine lettuce, the 1½ cups cucumber, mint, and basil. Pour the remaining ¼ cup ginger vinaigrette over lettuce; toss gently to coat.

5 To serve, divide rice sticks among four shallow bowls or dinner plates. Arrange lettuce and meat on top of rice sticks. Top with carrot, peanuts, additional cucumber, and cilantro. If desired, squeeze juice from lime wedges over salads.

PER SERVING 618 **CAL**; 37 g **FAT** (6 g **SAT**); 35 mg **CHOL**; 428 mg **SODIUM**; 53 g **CARB**; 3 g **FIBER**; 19 g **PRO**

Cheese-Stuffed Knockwursts

Knockwurst is a garlicky German sausage with a crisp skin that snaps when you bite into it. If you can't find it, bratwurst makes a perfectly acceptable substitute.

MAKES 5 servings **PREP** 15 minutes **GRILL** 8 minutes

5	**cooked knockwurst or bratwurst (about 1 pound)**
2	**ounces Monterey Jack cheese with caraway seeds***
¼	**cup thinly sliced green onions (2)**
5	**slices bacon**
5	**French-style rolls or frankfurter buns, split** **Ketchup, mustard, pickle relish, and/or** **crumbled crisp-cooked bacon (optional)**

1 Cut a lengthwise slit, about ½ inch deep, in each knockwurst. Cut cheese into five 2½ x ½ x ¼-inch strips. Insert a cheese strip and a scant 1 tablespoon green onions into each slit. Wrap a slice of bacon around each knockwurst; secure with wooden toothpicks.

2 For a charcoal grill, arrange medium-hot coals around a drip pan. Test for medium heat above pan. Place knockwurst, cheese sides up, on a grill rack over drip pan. Cover and grill for 8 to 10 minutes or until bacon is crisp and cheese is melted. (For a gas grill, preheat grill. Reduce heat to medium. Adjust for indirect cooking. Place knockwurst on grill rack over the burner that is turned off. Grill as directed.)

3 Remove and discard toothpicks from knockwurst. Serve knockwurst in rolls. If desired, top with ketchup, mustard, pickle relish, and/or additional bacon.

***Tip** Or use regular Monterey Jack cheese and sprinkle with a few caraway seeds.

PER SERVING 473 **CAL**; 34 g **FAT** (13 g **SAT**); 77 mg **CHOL**; 1,129 mg **SODIUM**; 21 g **CARB**; 1 g **FIBER**; 19 g **PRO**

Authentically Awesome Spare Ribs with Fig-Jalapeño Sauce

Floridian Dan LaBrie tasted his first fresh fig at a Napa Valley restaurant that happened to have a fig tree. Dan was awed by the flavor, and took it as a sign to use fresh figs in his next contest entry. That inspiration won him $5,000 in the 2012 Gnarly Head Ribs Recipe Contest.

MAKES 4 servings **PREP** 35 minutes **BAKE** 1 hour 45 minutes at 350°F
STAND 5 minutes **GRILL** 36 minutes

Butter-flavor nonstick cooking spray
4½ pounds pork spareribs, membrane removed
2 teaspoons salt
2 teaspoons black pepper
1 small onion, quartered
2 cloves garlic, smashed
1 cup organic vegetable broth
½ tablespoon olive oil
1 small fresh jalapeño (see tip, page 10)
¼ cup honey
¼ cup Gnarly Head® Authentic Red Wine
¼ cup fig preserves
¼ cup ketchup
1 teaspoon onion powder
½ teaspoon fine sea salt
4 ounces fresh Mission figs, stemmed
¼ cup cold water

1 Preheat oven to 350°F. Coat a roasting pan with nonstick spray; set aside. Sprinkle ribs with salt and pepper. Rub in with your fingers. Add ribs to prepared pan. Add onion, garlic, and vegetable broth on top of ribs. Cover with aluminum foil; bake for 1¾ to 2 hours or until the meat starts to pull away from the bone.

2 Meanwhile, brush the jalapeño with olive oil. For a charcoal or gas grill, place jalapeño on a grill rack directly over medium heat. Cover and grill for 8 to 10 minutes or until all sides are charred. Remove from heat; let cool. Seed and set aside.

3 In a medium saucepan combine honey, the Gnarly Head® Authentic Red Wine, fig preserves, ketchup, onion powder, and sea salt. Bring to boiling; reduce heat and simmer, uncovered, for 15 minutes. Keep warm.

4 Remove ribs from oven; let rest for about 5 minutes. For charcoal grill, arrange medium-hot coals around a drip pan. Test for medium heat above pan. Place ribs, bone side up, on grill rack over drip pan. Cover and grill 20 minutes, turning once halfway through. (For a gas grill, preheat grill. Reduce heat to medium. Adjust for indirect cooking. Place ribs on grill rack over burner that is off. Grill as directed.)

5 Meanwhile, in a blender or food processor, combine roasted jalapeño and figs. Cover and blend or process until combined. Add the jalapeño mixture and the cold water to the saucepan with the honey mixture. Bring to boiling reduce heat and simmer, uncovered, about 2 minutes.

6 Turn the ribs bone side up. Baste with half the fig-jalapeño sauce. Cover and grill for 4 minutes. Turn the ibs and baste with remaining sauce. Cover and grill for 4 to 5 minutes.

PER SERVING 1,143 **CAL**; 80 g **FAT** (26 g **SAT**); 281 mg **CHOL**; 1,815 mg **SODIUM**; 42 g **CARB**; 2 g **FIBER**; 56 g **PRO**

Bricked Chicken with Grilled Oranges

Removing the backbone to flatten a whole chicken is called spatchcocking. A flattened bird cooks much more quickly than an intact one. Weighting it with a brick allows the skin more contact with the heat—which means crisper skin.

MAKES 4 servings **PREP** 25 minutes **MARINATE** 2 hours **GRILL** 50 minutes

1	3- to 3½-pound whole roasting chicken
1¼	cups orange juice
1	cup lemon juice (juice of 5 or 6 lemons)
¼	cup olive oil
¼	cup snipped fresh parsley
1	tablespoon garlic powder
1	tablespoon onion powder
1	tablespoon black pepper
1	tablespoon kosher salt
1	recipe Citrus Rub
1	medium orange, cut into wedges

1 Remove the neck and giblets from chicken. Place chicken, breast side down, on a cutting board. Starting from the neck end, use scissors to cut lengthwise along one side of the backbone. Repeat the lengthwise cut on the opposite side of the backbone. Remove and discard the backbone. Turn chicken cut side down. Flatten the chicken as much as possible with your hands. Use kitchen shears to remove the wing tips.

2 For marinade, in a bowl combine orange juice, lemon juice, olive oil, parsley, garlic powder, onion powder, pepper, and salt.

3 Place chicken in a resealable plastic bag set in a large shallow dish. Pour the marinade over chicken. Seal bag; turn to coat chicken. Marinate in the refrigerator for 2 hours and up to 4 hours, turning the bag occasionally. Drain chicken, discarding marinade. Pat chicken dry with paper towels.

4 Starting at the neck on one side of the breast, slip your fingers between skin and meat, loosening skin as you work downward. Free the skin around the thigh. Repeat on the other side. With fingers spread Citrus Rub all over and under the skin of the chicken.

5 For a charcoal grill, arrange medium-hot coals around a drip pan. Test for medium heat above pan. Place chicken, breast side down, on grill rack over drip pan. Weight with two foil-wrapped bricks or a large cast-iron skillet. Grill for 30 minutes.

6 Turn chicken breast side up on rack, weighting again with bricks or skillet. Continue to cook, covered, about 20 minutes or until a thermometer registers 180°F for thigh. Add orange wedges to grill the last 10 minutes of grilling time. (For a gas grill, preheat grill. Reduce heat to medium. Place chicken on grill rack over heat. Cover; grill as above.) Squeeze orange wedges over chicken.

Citrus Rub In a small bowl combine 2 tablespoons olive oil, 2 tablespoons finely shredded orange and/or lemon peel, 1 tablespoon chopped fresh parsley, 1 tablespoon honey, 1 teaspoon kosher salt, and 1 teaspoon black pepper.

PER SERVING 649 **CAL**; 46 g **FAT** (11 g **SAT**); 173 mg **CHOL**; 1,097 mg **SODIUM**; 15 g **CARB**; 2 g **FIBER**; 44 g **PRO**

Cranberry-Chipotle Drumsticks

Just four ingredients make a mighty flavorful meal. Serve these spicy, smoky drumsticks with mashed sweet potatoes.

MAKES 6 servings **PREP** 15 minutes **GRILL** 35 minutes

1	**16-ounce can whole cranberry sauce**
½	**cup barbecue sauce**
1	**canned chipotle pepper in adobo sauce, finely chopped (see tip, page 10)**
12	**chicken drumsticks or 6 skinless, boneless chicken breast halves**

1 In a medium bowl stir together cranberry sauce, barbecue sauce, and chipotle pepper. For dipping sauce, pour 1 cup of the cranberry-chipotle sauce into a serving bowl; cover and chill. For basting sauce, transfer the remaining sauce to a blender or food processor. Cover and blend until smooth.

2 For a charcoal or gas grill, place chicken on the grill rack directly over medium heat. Cover and grill until chicken is no longer pink, turning once halfway through grilling and brushing with basting sauce during the last 5 minutes of grilling. Allow 35 to 45 minutes for drumsticks (180°F) or 12 to 15 minutes for breast halves (170°F). Discard basting sauce. Serve chicken with reserved cranberry-chipotle dipping sauce.

PER SERVING 371 **CAL**; 12 g **FAT** (3 g **SAT**); 95 mg **CHOL**; 415 mg **SODIUM**; 36 g **CARB**; 1 g **FIBER**; 28 g **PRO**

Spicy Grilled Shrimp

Sprinkle the cooked shrimp and rice with sliced scallions for a fresh crunch.

MAKES 6 servings **PREP** 15 minutes **MARINATE** 1 hour
GRILL 7 minutes

- 1½ **pounds fresh or frozen, peeled and deveined extra-large shrimp**
- ¼ **cup low-sugar orange marmalade**
- ¼ **cup honey**
- 2 **to 3 teaspoons Cajun seasoning**
- 1 **tablespoon olive oil**
- 2 **cups hot cooked rice**

1 Thaw shrimp, if frozen. If using wooden skewers, soak in water for 1 hour. Rinse shrimp; pat dry. For sauce, in a small saucepan stir together marmalade, honey, and ½ teaspoon of the Cajun seasoning; set aside.

2 Place shrimp in a resealable plastic bag set in a shallow bowl. For marinade, in a small bowl combine oil and remaining Cajun seasoning. Pour marinade over shrimp. Seal bag; turn to coat shrimp. Marinate in refrigerator for 1 hour, turning bag occasionally.

3 Drain shrimp, discarding marinade. Thread shrimp onto skewers. For a charcoal or gas grill, place kabobs on the greased rack of a grill directly over medium heat. Cover and grill for 7 to 9 minutes or until shrimp are opaque, turning once halfway through grilling.

4 Stir marmalade sauce over low heat for 2 to 3 minutes or until melted. Drizzle sauce over kabobs and serve with hot cooked rice.

PER SERVING 267 **CAL**; 4 g **FAT** (1 g **SAT**); 172 mg **CHOL**; 231 mg **SODIUM**; 31 g **CARB**; 1 g **FIBER**; 25 g **PRO**

Grilled Salmon and Asparagus with Garden Mayonnaise

An herbed mayo studded with celery and green onions is a creamy-crunchy topping for this super simple grilled salmon.

MAKES 4 servings **PREP** 10 minutes **GRILL** 8 minutes

- 4 **6- to 8-ounce fresh or frozen skinless salmon fillets, about 1 inch thick**
- 1 **pound asparagus spears**
- 1 **tablespoon olive oil**
  Salt and black pepper
- ½ **cup finely chopped celery (1 stalk)**
- ⅓ **cup mayonnaise**
- ¼ **cup thinly sliced green onions (2)**
- 1 **tablespoon lemon juice**
- 2 **teaspoons snipped fresh tarragon**
  Lemon wedges (optional)

1 Thaw fish, if frozen. Rinse fish; pat dry with paper towels. Snap off and discard woody bases from asparagus. Brush both sides of fish and asparagus lightly with olive oil. Sprinkle fish and asparagus with salt and pepper.

2 For a charcoal or gas grill, place fish and asparagus on the greased grill rack directly over medium heat. Cover and grill for 8 to 12 minutes or until fish begins to flake when tested with a fork and asparagus is tender, turning fish once, and turning asparagus occasionally.

3 Meanwhile, for garden mayonnaise, in a small bowl stir together celery, mayonnaise, green onions, lemon juice, and tarragon. Chill until serving time.

4 To serve, arrange fish and asparagus on four dinner plates. Top fish with garden mayonnaise. If desired, serve with lemon wedges.

PER SERVING 545 **CAL**; 41 g **FAT** (8 g **SAT**); 100 mg **CHOL**; 314 mg **SODIUM**; 6 g **CARB**; 3 g **FIBER**; 37 g **PRO**

GRILLED SALMON AND ASPARAGUS
WITH GARDEN MAYONNAISE

Grilled Vegetable Pizza

Grilling gives the vegetables delicious smoky flavor and the crusts tasty charring. Then they are arranged on crusts and grilled again to finish the pizzas and melt the cheese.

MAKES 6 servings **PREP** 25 minutes **STAND** 15 minutes **GRILL** 15 minutes

⅔ cup warm water (120°F to 130°F)
1   package fast-rising active dry yeast
½   teaspoon sugar
¾   cup whole wheat flour
¾   cup all-purpose flour
½   teaspoon salt
2   tablespoons olive oil
1   tablespoon yellow cornmeal
1   medium yellow summer squash, cut lengthwise into thirds
1   medium red sweet pepper, quartered
8   ounces asparagus spears, trimmed
8   ounces portobello mushrooms
¼   cup garlic hummus
½   teaspoon kosher salt
¼   teaspoon freshly ground black pepper
2   ounces provolone cheese, shredded (½ cup)

1 In a small bowl combine the water, yeast, and sugar; let stand for 5 minutes. In a medium bowl combine whole wheat flour, all-purpose flour, and ½ teaspoon salt. Using a wooden spoon, stir in yeast mixture and 1 tablespoon of the olive oil until combined.

2 Turn dough out onto a lightly floured surface. Knead dough for 6 to 8 minutes to make a moderately stiff dough that is smooth and elastic. Cover; let rest for 15 to 20 minutes.

3 Punch dough down; divide in half. On a lightly floured surface, roll out each half into an 11 x 7-inch oval. Sprinkle cornmeal on a large baking sheet. Place pizza crusts on baking sheet; set aside.

4 In a very large bowl drizzle summer squash, red sweet pepper, asparagus, and mushrooms with the remaining 1 tablespoon olive oil. Toss to coat.

5 For a charcoal or gas grill, grill vegetables on the rack of a covered grill directly over medium heat for 8 to 10 minutes or until tender and lightly charred, turning once and removing vegetables from the grill as they are done. Cut vegetables into 1- to 2-inch pieces. (If desired, remove skin from sweet pepper.)

6 Grill pizza crusts on the rack of a covered grill directly over medium heat for 3 or 4 minutes or until bottoms are lightly charred. Transfer crusts to the baking sheet, charred side up. Spread 2 tablespoons hummus over each crust. Top evenly with grilled vegetables. Sprinkle vegetables evenly with ½ teaspoon kosher salt, the pepper, and provolone cheese. Return pizzas to grill rack. Cover and grill about 4 minutes more or until bottoms of crusts are crisp and lightly charred. Transfer pizzas to a cutting board; cut each into three pieces.

PER SERVING 240 **CAL**; 9 g **FAT** (3 g **SAT**); 7 mg **CHOL**; 531 mg **SODIUM**; 32 g **CARB**; 5 g **FIBER**; 10 g **PRO**

GRILLED VEGETABLE PIZZA

healthy favorites

Delicious, healthful recipes that keep you on track.

SPAGHETTI PIE

Chipotle-Picante Meat Loaf with Cilantro

Nutritious, high fiber ground flaxseed meal keeps this lean and flavorful meat loaf in shape.

MAKES 4 servings **PREP** 20 minutes **BAKE** 40 minutes at 350°F **STAND** 10 minutes

Nonstick cooking spray
- ⅔ **cup chipotle salsa**
- ¼ **cup refrigerated or frozen egg product, thawed**
- ½ **10-ounce package frozen cooked brown rice, thawed (about 1½ cups)**
- 2 **tablespoons ground flaxseed meal**
- ¾ **cup chopped fresh cilantro**
- ¼ **teaspoon salt**
- 1 **pound extra-lean ground beef**

1 Preheat oven to 350°F. Coat a foil-lined baking pan with cooking spray.

2 In a large mixing bowl combine ⅓ cup of the salsa, the egg product, rice, flaxseed, cilantro, and salt; add ground beef and mix well. Shape into an oval loaf (about 8 inches long by 5 inches wide). Place in prepared pan. Bake, uncovered, for 40 to 45 minutes or until an instant-read thermometer registers 160°F. Let stand 10 minutes before slicing.

3 To serve, spoon remaining ⅓ cup salsa on meat loaf slices.

PER SERVING 256 **CAL**; 8 g **FAT** (3 g **SAT**); 70 mg **CHOL**; 470 mg **SODIUM**; 15 g **CARB**; 2 g **FIBER**; 28 g **PRO**

Southwestern Beef, Rice, and Black Bean Salad

If you're using wooden skewers, soak them in water for 1 hour before threading the meat and onions to prevent them from burning.

MAKES 6 servings **PREP** 45 minutes **GRILL** 4 minutes

1	pound beef top sirloin steak, cut 1 inch thick
2	teaspoons salt-free Southwest seasoning blend
1	teaspoon olive oil
4	green onions, cut into 1-inch lengths
12	6- to 8-inch skewers
1½	cups cooked brown rice
1	15-ounce can no-salt-added black beans, rinsed and drained
½	cup chopped, seeded tomato (1 medium)
¼	cup snipped fresh cilantro
1	cup frozen whole kernel corn
¾	cup chopped green sweet pepper (1 medium)
½	cup chopped sweet onion (1 small)
2	teaspoons olive oil
½	cup bottled salsa
¼	cup lime juice
½	teaspoon ground cumin

1 Cut steak into 2 x ¼-inch strips. In a medium bowl toss steak, seasoning blend, and the 1 teaspoon olive oil. Thread steak strips and green onions evenly onto skewers; set aside.

2 For salad, in a large bowl combine rice, black beans, tomato, and cilantro; set aside. In a large nonstick skillet cook corn, sweet pepper, and sweet onion in the 2 teaspoons olive oil over medium-high heat for 5 minutes or until corn is slightly blackened, stirring frequently. Add to rice mixture. In a small bowl stir together salsa, lime juice, and cumin. Add to rice mixture; toss to combine. Set salad aside.

3 For a charcoal or gas grill, place kabobs on a grill rack directly over medium heat. Cover and grill for 4 to 6 minutes or just until meat is pink in the center, turning once halfway through grilling.

4. Serve spoon beef kabobs with black bean salad.

PER SERVING 271 **CAL**; 6 g **FAT** (2 g **SAT**); 45 mg **CHOL**; 185 mg **SODIUM**; 32 g **CARB**; 6 g **FIBER**; 23 g **PRO**

Roasted Pork with Blackberry Sauce

The flavor of pork pairs particularly well with fruit—apples, apricots, peaches, plums, and berries of all kinds. The blackberry spreadable fruit in this recipe serves as a base for a sauce flavored with wine, balsamic vinegar, mustard, garlic, soy sauce, orange peel, and rosemary.

MAKES 6 servings **PREP** 20 minutes **MARINATE** 2 hours **ROAST** 35 minutes at 425°F **STAND** 10 minutes

1½ **pounds pork tenderloin**
¼   **cup blackberry spreadable fruit, melted and cooled**
¼   **cup dry white wine or apple juice**
2   **tablespoons balsamic vinegar**
2   **tablespoons olive oil**
2   **tablespoons Dijon mustard**
3   **cloves garlic, minced**
1   **teaspoon reduced-sodium soy sauce**
1   **teaspoon finely shredded orange peel**
½   **teaspoon snipped fresh rosemary**
    Finely shredded orange peel (optional)
    Steamed green beans (optional)

1 Place tenderloin in a resealable plastic bag set in a shallow dish. For marinade, in a bowl whisk together spreadable fruit, wine, balsamic vinegar, olive oil, mustard, garlic, soy sauce, 1 teaspoon orange peel, and rosemary. Pour marinade over pork; seal bag. Marinate, refrigerated, 2 to 5 hours, turning bag occasionally.

2 Preheat oven to 425°F. Drain pork, reserving marinade. Place meat on a rack in a shallow roasting pan. Roast 30 to 35 minutes or until thermometer registers 145°F. Remove from oven; loosely cover and let stand for 10 minutes.

3 Meanwhile, for sauce, in a small saucepan bring reserved marinade to boiling; reduce heat. Simmer, uncovered, 5 minutes. Slice pork; serve with sauce and, if desired, top with additional orange peel and serve with green beans.

*Tip For a charcoal grill, arrange medium-hot coals around a drip pan. Test for medium heat above pan. Place meat on grill rack over drip pan. Cover and grill for 30 to 35 minutes or until thermometer registers 145°F. (For a gas grill, preheat grill. Reduce heat to medium. Adjust for indirect cooking. Grill as above.) Remove meat from grill; loosely cover and let stand for 10 minutes. Prepare sauce as directed above.

PER SERVING 211 **CAL**; 7 g **FAT** (1 g **SAT**); 74 mg **CHOL**; 211 mg **SODIUM**; 9 g **CARB**; 24 g **PRO**

Lemon-Hoisin Glazed Chicken on Asparagus and Cherry Sesame Rice

Californian Merry Graham is used to thinking creatively about food. As a volunteer at a local church preparing meals for those in need , she was given day-old produce donated by food vendors and then cooked up a meal based on those ingredients. That creativity helped her win the $10,000 grand prize for this Asian-inspired recipe in the 2012 Foster Farms® Fresh Chicken Cooking Contest.

MAKES 6 servings   **PREP** 20 minutes   **COOK** 50 minutes

6	**Foster Farms skinless, boneless chicken thighs, cut into 1-inch pieces**
1	**tablespoon grated fresh ginger**
4	**cloves garlic, minced**
¾	**teaspoon salt**
3	**tablespoons peanut oil**
1½	**cups jasmine rice, rinsed and drained**
6	**green onions, chopped, white and green parts divided**
2	**cups reduced-sodium chicken broth**
2	**teaspoons finely shredded lemon peel**
¼	**cup lemon juice**
⅔	**cup dried tart cherries, snipped**
1	**tablespoon toasted sesame oil**
⅓	**cup rice vinegar**
¼	**cup hoisin sauce**
1½	**tablespoons honey**
½	**teaspoon crushed red pepper**
2	**teaspoons black sesame seeds**
1	**pound fresh asparagus spears, trimmed and cut into 2-inch pieces**
½	**cup snipped fresh cilantro**
⅓	**cup roasted salted almonds, coarsely chopped**

1 In a medium bowl combine chicken, ginger, half the garlic, and ½ teaspoon salt. Set aside.

2 In a medium saucepan heat 1 tablespoon of the peanut oil over medium heat. Add jasmine rice, onion whites, and remaining garlic. Cook, stirring frequently, for 8 minutes or until beginning to toast. Add broth, 2 tablespoons of the lemon juice, and ¼ teaspoon salt; bring to boiling. Cover, reduce heat to low, and cook 15 minutes. Uncover, fluff with a fork, stir in dried cherries, sesame oil, and remaining green onions. Set aside.

3 In a large skillet heat 1 tablespoon of the peanut oil over medium-high heat. Add chicken mixture and cook, stirring frequently, for 6 minutes or until no longer pink on the outside.

4 For sauce, in small bowl stir together vinegar, hoisin, 1 tablespoon of the honey, the remaining 2 tablespoons lemon juice, 1 teaspoon lemon peel ,and ¼ teaspoon crushed red pepper. Add sauce to chicken in pan and continue cooking for 10 minutes on medium heat. Increase heat to high and cook 2 to 4 minutes until sauce on chicken is dark and has thickened. Sprinkle chicken with black sesame seeds. Remove pan from heat, set aside and keep warm.

5 In another large skillet heat remaining 1 tablespoon peanut oil over high heat. Add asparagus, and remaining honey, and ¼ teaspoon crushed red pepper. Cook, stirring frequently, for 2 to 4 minutes, or until asparagus is tender. If desired, season to taste with salt.

6 To serve, place rice on serving platter. Top with half the cilantro, the almonds, and then roasted asparagus. Top with chicken pieces. Sprinkle with remaining cilantro and remaining 1 teaspoon lemon peel.

PER SERVING 512 **CAL**; 17 g **FAT** (3 g **SAT**); 66 mg **CHOL**; 645 mg **SODIUM**; 68 g **CARB**; 4 g **FIBER**; 22 g **PRO**

Chicken, Potato, and Gravy Bowls

Comfort food doesn't have to destroy your diet—and this dish is proof. Juicy skinless chicken thighs are shredded and layered on lightened-up garlic mashed potatoes, then topped with reduced-sodium gravy.

MAKES 4 servings **PREP** 15 minutes **COOK** 34 minutes

1½	**pounds Yukon gold potatoes or other potatoes, quartered**
1	**tablespoon canola oil**
12	**ounces skinless boneless chicken thighs**
2	**teaspoons bottled minced roasted garlic**
¼	**cup light sour cream**
¼	**cup fat free milk**
2	**teaspoons snipped fresh thyme or parsley**
¼	**teaspoon salt**
⅛	**teaspoon black pepper**
1	**7- to 8-ounce 30% less sodium brown gravy mix**
	Sprigs fresh thyme or parsley (optional)

1 In a large saucepan cook potatoes, covered, in a small amount of boiling water for 20 to 25 minutes or until tender.

2 Meanwhile, in a large skillet heat oil over medium-high heat. Reduce heat to medium; add chicken thighs. Cook 14 to 18 minutes, or until no longer pink, turning once halfway through cooking time. Coarsely shred chicken. Cover and keep warm.

3 Drain cooked potatoes; return to saucepan. Add garlic to potatoes. Mash with a potato masher or an electric mixer on low. Add sour cream, milk, the 2 teaspoons thyme, the salt, and pepper. Mash until light and fluffy. Cover and keep warm.

4 Prepare gravy mix according to package directions. To serve, in bowls layer potatoes, and chicken; top with gravy. Garnish servings with a thyme sprig, if desired.

PER SERVING 312 **CAL**; 9 g **FAT** (2 g **SAT**); 75 mg **CHOL**; 480 mg **SODIUM**; 35 g **CARB**; 4 g **FIBER**; 22 g **PRO**

Italian Roasted Chicken and Vegetable Toss

Add a couple of extra chicken breasts to the roasting pan when making this dish. Use the 2 cooked breasts the recipe calls for—and save the others for topping healthful salads and filling sandwiches the rest of the week.

MAKES 6 servings **PREP** 25 minutes
BAKE 50 minutes at 375°F

	Nonstick cooking spray
2	**bone-in chicken breast halves (2 pounds total)**
1	**cup packaged peeled baby carrots**
1	**medium onion, cut into 8 wedges**
2	**medium zucchini, cut into 1-inch chunks (3 cups)**
1	**medium red or green sweet pepper, cut into 1-inch chunks (about 1 cup)**
8	**ounces fresh mushrooms**
3	**tablespoons olive oil**
¼	**each teaspoon salt and black pepper**
2	**tablespoons balsamic vinegar**
1	**teaspoon dried Italian seasoning, crushed**
8	**ounces Mediterranean blend salad greens (8 cups)**
¼	**cup shredded Parmesan cheese (1 ounce)**

1 Preheat oven to 375°F. Coat a shallow roasting pan with cooking spray. Arrange chicken breast halves, skin sides up, in one half of the pan. Arrange carrots and onion in the opposite half. Bake, uncovered, for 25 minutes.

2 Remove pan from oven. Add zucchini, sweet pepper, and mushrooms to vegetables in pan. Drizzle chicken and vegetables with 2 tablespoons of the oil. Toss vegetables to coat. Sprinkle chicken and vegetables with salt and pepper.

3 Bake, uncovered, about 25 minutes more or until chicken is no longer pink (170°F) and vegetables are tender. Remove and set aside until chicken is cool enough to handle (5 to 10 minutes). Transfer vegetables to a large bowl.

4 Remove and discard skin and bones from chicken. Using two forks, pull chicken apart into big shreds. Add chicken and any juices in pan to vegetables; toss. In a small bowl whisk together vinegar, the remaining 1 tablespoon olive oil, and the Italian seasoning. Add to chicken mixture and toss to coat.

5 Arrange salad greens on a serving platter. Spoon chicken and vegetables on greens. Sprinkle with cheese.

PER SERVING 219 **CAL**; 10 g **FAT** (2 g **SAT**); 51 mg **CHOL**; 217 mg **SODIUM**; 10 g **CARB**; 2 g **FIBER**; 22 g **PRO**

ITALIAN ROASTED CHICKEN
AND VEGETABLE TOSS

Mango Chicken Salad with Coconut

Watch the coconut carefully as it toasts in the oven—it burns very easily!

MAKES 4 servings **PREP** 25 minutes
BAKE 4 minutes at 350°F

3   skinless, boneless chicken breast halves
2   limes
1   cup unsweetened coconut milk
1   tablespoon soy sauce
½   teaspoon crushed red pepper
½   cup flaked unsweetened coconut
2   mangoes, seeded, peeled, and chopped
    Lettuce leaves (optional)

1 Preheat oven to 350°F. Cut chicken into bite-size chunks. Squeeze juice from 1 lime (about 2 tablespoons juice); cut remaining lime into wedges.

2 In a large saucepan combine coconut milk, the lime juice, soy sauce, and crushed red pepper. Add chicken and bring to boiling; reduce heat and cook, covered, for 12 to 15 minutes or until chicken is cooked through, stirring occasionally.

3 Meanwhile, spread flaked coconut in a shallow pan. Bake, uncovered, for 4 to 5 minutes or until golden, stirring once.

4 Transfer chicken and cooking liquid to a bowl. Add mangoes; toss to coat. Sprinkle with toasted coconut. Spoon onto lettuce leaves to serve. Pass lime wedges.

PER SERVING 302 **CAL**; 10 g **FAT** (7 g **SAT**); 62 mg **CHOL**; 381 mg **SODIUM**; 29 g **CARB**; 4 g **FIBER**; 27 g **PRO**

Spaghetti Pie

Serve this kid-friendly pasta pie with a crisp green salad.

MAKES 6 servings **PREP** 35 minutes
BAKE 25 minutes at 350°F **STAND** 15 minutes

    Nonstick cooking spray
4   ounces dried spaghetti
2   egg whites, lightly beaten
⅓   cup grated Parmesan cheese
1   tablespoon olive oil
2   egg whites, lightly beaten
1   12-ounce container low-fat cottage cheese, drained (1¼ cups)
8   ounces uncooked ground turkey breast or 90% or higher lean ground beef
1   cup sliced fresh mushrooms
½   cup chopped onion
½   cup chopped green and/or red sweet pepper
2   cloves garlic, minced
1   8-ounce can no-salt-added tomato sauce
1½ teaspoons dried Italian seasoning, crushed
⅛   teaspoon salt
½   cup shredded part-skim mozzarella cheese (2 ounces)

1 Preheat oven to 350°F. Coat a 9-inch pie plate with nonstick cooking spray; set aside. For crust, cook spaghetti according to package directions, except omit the cooking oil and salt. Meanwhile, in a medium bowl stir together 2 egg whites, the Parmesan cheese, and olive oil. Drain spaghetti well; add to egg white mixture and toss to coat. Press spaghetti mixture into the bottom and up the sides of the prepared pie plate; set aside.

2 In a small bowl stir together 2 egg whites and drained cottage cheese. Spread over the crust in pie plate. Set aside.

3 In a large skillet cook turkey, mushrooms, onion, sweet pepper, and garlic until meat is browned. Drain off fat. Stir tomato sauce, Italian seasoning, and salt into meat mixture in skillet. Spoon over cottage cheese layer in crust.

4 Bake for 20 minutes or until heated through. Sprinkle with mozzarella cheese. Bake for 5 minutes or until cheese is melted. Let stand for 15 minutes. Cut into wedges to serve.

PER SERVING 256 **CAL**; 7 g **FAT** (3 g **SAT**); 27 mg **CHOL**; 479 mg **SODIUM**; 23 g **CARB**; 2 g **FIBER**; 26 g **PRO**

SPAGHETTI PIE

Dijon Lentil and Sausage Casserole

This casserole is both rustic and elegant—and a delicious way to warm up on a cold winter night. A sprinkle of gremolata—a mixture of lemon peel, parsley, and garlic—adds color and bright flavor right before serving.

MAKES 8 servings   **PREP** 40 minutes   **BAKE** 35 minutes at 400°F

1	**14.5-ounce can reduced-sodium chicken broth**
1	**cup water**
8	**ounces fresh green beans, trimmed and cut into 2- to 3-inch pieces (about 2 cups)**
2	**medium parsnips, peeled and cut into ½-inch slices**
3	**medium shallots, halved, or 1 medium onion, cut into thin wedges**
8	**ounces smoked cooked turkey sausage, coarsely chopped**
1¼	**cups red lentils, rinsed and drained**
⅓	**cup dry white wine or reduced-sodium chicken broth**
2	**tablespoons Dijon mustard**
2	**teaspoons snipped fresh thyme or ½ teaspoon dried thyme, crushed**
4	**cloves garlic, minced**
1½	**cups coarse soft whole wheat bread crumbs**
1	**tablespoon canola oil**
¼	**cup snipped fresh parsley**
2	**teaspoons finely shredded lemon peel**
	Lemon slices, halved, and/or fresh parsley sprigs (optional)

1 Preheat oven to 400°F. In a large saucepan combine broth and the water. Bring to boiling. Add green beans, parsnips, and shallots. Return to boiling; reduce heat. Simmer, covered, for 8 to 10 minutes or just until vegetables are tender. Remove from heat. Stir in sausage and lentils. In a small bowl combine wine, mustard, thyme, and half of the minced garlic; stir into sausage mixture.

2 Transfer sausage mixture to a 2-quart casserole. Bake, covered, for 25 to 30 minutes or just until lentils are tender.

3 Meanwhile, in a medium bowl toss together bread crumbs and oil. Sprinkle over casserole. Bake, uncovered, about 10 minutes more or until heated through and crumbs are lightly browned.

4 For gremolata, in a small bowl combine snipped parsley, lemon peel, and the remaining minced garlic. Sprinkle over casserole before serving. If desired, garnish with lemon slices and/or parsley sprigs.

PER SERVING 236 **CAL**; 5 g **FAT** (1 g **SAT**); 20 mg **CHOL**; 577 mg **SODIUM**; 31 g **CARB**; 12 g **FIBER**; 15 g **PRO**

Grilled Halibut with Blueberry-Pepper Sauce

A sage-infused antioxidant-rich blueberry sauce accompanies heart-healthy grilled fish in this dish.
Any meaty fish works well—halibut, sea bass, salmon, or cod.

MAKES 4 servings **PREP** 25 minutes **GRILL** 12 minutes

4	**5- to 6-ounce fresh or frozen halibut steaks or fillets or sea bass or salmon fillets, about 1 inch thick**
1½	**cups fresh blueberries, rinsed and drained**
1	**teaspoon chopped fresh sage**
½	**teaspoon freshly ground black pepper**
1	**cup garlic croutons, coarsely crushed**
¼	**cup chopped fresh sage**
1	**teaspoon finely shredded orange peel**
¼	**teaspoon freshly ground black pepper**
2	**tablespoons orange juice**
1	**tablespoon olive oil**
	Olive oil (optional)
	Fresh sage leaves (optional)

1 Thaw fish, if frozen. Rinse fish; pat dry with paper towels. For blueberry-pepper sauce, in a medium bowl use a potato masher or fork to mash ¾ cup of the blueberries. Stir in the remaining ¾ cup blueberries, the 1 teaspoon sage, and the ½ teaspoon pepper. Cover and chill until ready to serve.

2 In a small bowl combine crushed croutons, the ¼ cup sage, the 1 teaspoon orange peel, and the ¼ teaspoon pepper. Add orange juice and the 1 tablespoon olive oil, stirring until lightly moistened; set aside.

3 Lightly grease the rack of a grill. For a charcoal or gas grill, place fish, skin sides up if using fillets, on the rack of a grill directly over medium heat. Cover and grill for 5 minutes. Turn fish; gently press crouton mixture onto fish. Cover and grill for 7 to 10 minutes or until fish flakes easily when tested with a fork.

4 To serve, place fish on a serving platter. Serve with blueberry-pepper sauce. If desired, drizzle fish with additional olive oil and garnish with sage leaves.

PER SERVING 222 **CAL**; 7 g **FAT** (1 g **SAT**); 45 mg **CHOL**; 101 mg **SODIUM**; 8 g **CARB**; 1 g **FIBER**; 30 g **PRO**

Scallop Salad with Basil Vinaigrette

English cucumbers are longer and more slender than regular cucumbers. They have thin, delicate and skin and seeds so small, the cucumbers are considered seedless. They are most often sold shrink-wrapped in plastic to retain moisture.

MAKES 4 servings **START TO FINISH** 25 minutes

1   pound fresh or frozen sea scallops
¼   cup snipped fresh basil
3   tablespoons balsamic vinegar
2   tablespoons lemon juice
2   tablespoons olive oil
2   teaspoons Dijon mustard
½   teaspoon black pepper
      Nonstick cooking spray
6   cups torn mixed salad greens
3   plum tomatoes, seeded and chopped
1   medium red sweet pepper, seeded and chopped
1   cup fresh corn kernels or frozen whole kernel corn, thawed
½   medium English cucumber, chopped
2   tablespoons finely shredded Parmesan cheese

1 Thaw scallops, if frozen. Rinse scallops; pat dry with paper towels. For vinaigrette, in a screw-top jar combine basil, vinegar, lemon juice, oil, mustard, and ¼ teaspoon of the black pepper. Cover and shake well. Set aside.

2 Sprinkle scallops with the remaining ¼ teaspoon black pepper. Coat an large unheated nonstick skillet with cooking spray. Preheat over medium-high heat. Add scallops. Cook for 2 to 4 minutes or until scallops are opaque, turning once halfway through cooking.

3 Meanwhile, divide salad greens among 4 serving plates. In a large bowl combine tomatoes, sweet pepper, corn, and cucumber. Add half of the vinaigrette; toss to coat. Top greens with vegetables. Add scallops to salads and drizzle with some of the remaining vinaigrette. Pass the remaining vinaigrette. Sprinkle with Parmesan cheese.

PER SERVING 261 **CAL**; 9 g **FAT** (2 g **SAT**); 39 mg **CHOL**; 282 mg **SODIUM**; 21 g **CARB**; 4 g **FIBER**; 23 g **PRO**

Fajita-Style Quesadillas

For a full meal, serve these crisp and cheesy quesadillas with a bowl of soup or a salad.

MAKES 4 servings **START TO FINISH** 30 minutes

½   **medium red or green sweet pepper, seeded and cut into bite-size strips**

½   **medium onion, halved and thinly sliced**

1   **fresh serrano pepper, halved, seeded, and cut in thin strips (see tip, page 10)**

2   **teaspoons vegetable oil**

4   **6-inch white corn tortillas**
    Nonstick cooking spray

½   **cup shredded Monterey Jack cheese (2 ounces)**

2   **thin slices tomato, halved crosswise**

1   **tablespoon snipped fresh cilantro (optional)**
    Light sour cream (optional)
    Cilantro and lime wedges (optional)

1 In an extra-large skillet cook sweet pepper, onion, and serrano pepper in hot oil over medium-high heat for 3 to 5 minutes or just until vegetables are tender. Remove from heat.

2 Lightly coat one side of each tortilla with cooking spray. On the uncoated side of two tortillas, divide half the cheese. Top with half the sweet pepper mixture, tomato slices, the cilantro, remaining cheese, then remaining tortillas, coated sides up.

3 Cook quesadillas in same skillet over medium heat for 4 to 5 minutes per side, until cheese is melted and tortillas are lightly browned. Cut each quesadilla in 4 wedges. If desired, sprinkle with cilantro and serve with sour cream and lime wedges.

PER SERVING 122 **CAL**; 8 g **FAT** (2 g **SAT**); 24 mg **CHOL**; 82 mg **SODIUM**; 10 g **CARB**; 2 g **FIBER**; 4 g **PRO**

Chunky Vegetable-Lentil Soup

French green du Puy lentils (sometimes called "the caviar of lentils") are smaller than common brown lentils—but there are other differences too. They have a distinctive nutty, peppery flavor and hold their shape better when cooked.

MAKES 6 servings **PREP** 25 minutes **COOK** 30 minutes

1	tablespoon olive oil
1	medium onion, cut into thin rings
1	clove garlic, minced
1	cup dry green (French) lentils, rinsed and drained
1	pound whole small mushrooms (halve or quarter any large mushrooms)
2	cups thinly sliced carrots (4 medium)
1	cup chopped celery stalks (2)
4	cups water
1	14-ounce can vegetable broth
¼	teaspoon salt
¼	teaspoon black pepper
2	cups thinly sliced napa or red cabbage

1 In a 4-quart saucepan or Dutch oven heat oil over medium heat. Add onion and garlic; cook for 4 to 5 minutes or until onion is tender, stirring occasionally. Stir in lentils; cook and stir 1 minute.

2 Add mushrooms, carrots, celery, the water, vegetable broth, salt, and pepper. Bring to boiling. Reduce heat and simmer, covered, about 25 minutes or until lentils are tender.

3 Serve in soup bowls and top with cabbage.

PER SERVING 185 **CAL**; 3 g **FAT** (0 g sat. fat), 0 g **CHOL**; g 408 mg **SODIUM**; 30 g **CARB**; 13 g **FIBER**; 12 g **PRO**

Four Cheese Macaroni and Cheese

A few tricks employed in the making of this mac and cheese keep it healthful despite its decadent look and taste. Whole-grain macaroni is baked with low-fat cheese sauce that has a whole pureed butternut squash stirred into it!

MAKES 8 servings **PREP** 30 minutes **BAKE** 40 minutes + 25 minutes at 375°F

Nonstick cooking spray
- 1 **pound butternut squash, halved and seeded**
- 8 **ounces dried whole grain elbow macaroni (about 2 cups)**
- 4 **teaspoons butter**
- 2 **tablespoons all-purpose flour**
- ½ **teaspoon salt**
- ⅛ **teaspoon ground white pepper**
- 1 **cup fat-free milk**
- 2 **tablespoons semisoft cheese with garlic and fine herbs**
- ¾ **cup shredded part-skim mozzarella cheese (3 ounces)**
- ¾ **cup shredded reduced-fat sharp cheddar cheese (3 ounces)**
- 2 **ounces Muenster cheese, very thinly sliced**

1 Preheat oven to 375°F. Line a 15 x 10 x 1-inch baking pan with parchment paper; set aside. Coat a 2-quart square baking dish with cooking spray; set aside.

2 Coat the cut sides of the butternut squash with cooking spray; place squash, cut sides down, in the prepared baking pan. Bake 40 to 45 minutes or until squash is very tender and cooked through. Remove from oven; let stand until cool enough to handle. Scoop flesh from squash into a bowl; discard skin. Using a potato masher, mash the squash; set aside.

3 Meanwhile, cook pasta according to package directions. Drain well.

4 In a medium saucepan melt butter over medium heat. Whisk in flour, salt, and white pepper until combined. Add milk, whisking until smooth. Cook and stir until thickened and bubbly. Add semisoft cheese; whisk until cheese is melted. Stir in mashed squash. Add cooked pasta; stir until coated.

5 Spoon half of the pasta into the prepared baking dish. Evenly sprinkle half the mozzarella cheese and half the cheddar cheese on top of the pasta in baking dish. Arrange half the Muenster cheese over all. Repeat layers. Bake for 25 minutes or until bubbly and top is golden brown.

PER SERVING 266 **CAL**; 11 g **FAT** (6 g **SAT**); 26 mg **CHOL**; 402 mg **SODIUM**; 31 g **CARB**; 4 g **FIBER**; 13 g **PRO**

potluck pleasers

Perfect size recipes for neighborhood parties or family gatherings.

CHICKEN NOODLE CASSEROLE

Hamburger Cheese Bake

Take this noodly, beefy, creamy casserole to your next gathering and you will go home with an empty dish.

MAKES 8 servings **PREP** 25 minutes
BAKE 30 minutes at 350°F

	Nonstick cooking spray
12	ounces lean ground beef
½	cup chopped onion (1 medium)
1	15-ounce can tomato sauce
¼	teaspoon salt
¼	teaspoon garlic powder
¼	teaspoon ground black pepper
4	cups dried medium noodles (about 8 ounces)
1	cup cottage cheese
½	8-ounce package cream cheese, cubed and softened
¼	cup sour cream
⅓	cup sliced green onions (3)
¼	cup chopped green sweet pepper
2	tablespoons grated Parmesan cheese
	Fresh snipped parsley (optional)

1 Preheat oven to 350°F. Lightly coat a 2-quart rectangular baking dish with cooking spray; set aside. In a large skillet cook beef and onion over medium heat until meat is browned and onion is tender. Drain off fat; discard. Stir in the tomato sauce, salt, garlic powder, and black pepper. Remove from heat.

2 Meanwhile, cook noodles according to package directions; drain. In a medium bowl stir together the cottage cheese, cream cheese, sour cream, green onions, and sweet pepper.

3 Spread half of the noodles in the prepared baking dish. Top with half of the meat mixture, then all of the cottage cheese mixture, spreading evenly. Top with the remaining noodles and remaining meat mixture. Sprinkle evenly with Parmesan cheese.

4 Bake, uncovered, for 30 minutes or until heated through. Sprinkle with parsley, if desired.

PER SERVING 311 **CAL**; 15 g **FAT** (7 g **SAT**); 77 mg **CHOL**; 551 mg **SODIUM**; 26 g **CARB**; 2 g **FIBER**; 17 g **PRO**

Three-Pork Bolognese Joes

These delightfully sloppy sandwiches have a familiar form—saucy, seasoned ground meat served in a bun— but with distinctive Italian flavor.

MAKES 10 servings **PREP** 40 minutes
SLOW COOK 6 hours (low) or 3 hours (high) + 20 minutes (high)

1	pound ground pork
8	ounces bulk Italian sausage
4	ounces pancetta or bacon, chopped
1	cup chopped onion (1 large)
3	cloves garlic, minced
1	cup chopped carrots (2 medium)
½	cup chopped celery (1 stalk)
½	cup chopped red sweet pepper (1 small)
½	cup dry red wine or chicken broth
¼	cup tomato paste
½	teaspoon salt
½	teaspoon ground thyme
¼	teaspoon crushed red pepper
½	cup whole milk
¼	cup chopped fresh parsley
10	ciabatta rolls, split
	Assorted toppings such as fresh mozzarella cheese slices, shredded fresh basil leaves, and/or roasted red sweet peppers, cut into chunks (optional)

1 In an extra-large skillet cook ground pork, sausage, pancetta, onion, and garlic over medium heat until meat is browned and onion is tender, using a wooden spoon to break up meat as it cooks. Drain off fat.

2 In a 3½- or 4-quart slow cooker combine meat mixture, carrots, celery, and sweet pepper. In a small bowl combine wine, tomato paste, salt, thyme, and crushed red pepper; add to cooker.

3 Cover and cook on low-heat setting for 6 to 8 hours or on high-heat setting for 3 to 4 hours. If using low heat, turn cook to high-heat setting. Add milk and parsley; stir. Cover and cook on high-heat setting for 20 minutes.

4 Use a slotted spoon to scoop meat into rolls. If desired, add toppings.

PER SERVING 547 **CAL**; 23 g **FAT** (9 g **SAT**); 64 mg **CHOL**; 1,087 mg **SODIUM**; 6 g **CARB**; 3 g **FIBER**; 24 g **PRO**

THREE-PORK BOLOGNESE JOES

Mexican Mac and Cheese

Whip up this dish for a weeknight supper or potluck party. With just 20 minutes of prep time, you can get it in the oven in a flash—then attend to other things while it bakes.

MAKES 12 servings **PREP** 20 minutes **BAKE** 35 minutes at 350°F **STAND** 10 minutes

12	**ounces dried mostaccioli or rigatoni pasta (3 cups)**
1	**pound bulk pork sausage**
1	**cup chopped onion (1 large)**
1	**16-ounce jar green medium-hot salsa**
4	**cups shredded Monterey Jack cheese (8 ounces)**
	Tomato wedges, sliced fresh jalapeño (see tip, page 10), and chopped fresh cilantro
	Salsa (optional)

1 Preheat oven to 350°F. Lightly grease a 3-quart rectangular baking dish; set aside. Cook pasta according to package directions. Drain; set aside.

2 Meanwhile, in a large skillet cook sausage and onion until meat is browned and onion is tender. Drain off fat; . Stir in green salsa.

3 In prepared baking dish layer half of the cooked pasta, half the sausage mixture, and half the cheese. Repeat layers. Bake, uncovered, for 35 minutes or until bubbly. Let stand 10 minutes. Top with tomato, jalapeño, and cilantro. If desired, serve with additional salsa.

PER SERVING 378 **CAL**; 22 g **FAT** (11 g **SAT**); 61 mg **CHOL**; 474 mg **SODIUM**; 25 g **CARB**; 1 g **FIBER**; 19 g **PRO**

Chicken Noodle Casserole

When it's cold and rainy, when the chips are down, or when you've simply had a hard day, feed your body and soul with this old-fashioned favorite.

MAKES 8 servings **PREP** 15 minutes **COOK** 35 minutes **BAKE** 30 minutes at 375°F

2	cups chopped celery (4 stalks)
½	cup chopped onion (1 medium)
2	teaspoons canola oil
2	pounds chicken legs and/or thighs, skinned
½	teaspoon black pepper
¾	teaspoon salt
1	teaspoon dried thyme, crushed
6	cups water
1	slice bread
10	ounces jumbo or extra-large egg noodles
1	8-ounce carton light sour cream
2	tablespoons flour
½	teaspoon garlic powder
	Nonstick cooking spray
2	tablespoons snipped fresh parsley

1 Preheat oven to 375°F. In a Dutch oven cook 1½ cups of the celery and ⅓ cup of the onion in hot oil over medium heat for 3 minutes. Add chicken, pepper, salt, and thyme to Dutch oven; cook for 2 minutes. Add the water. Bring to boiling; reduce heat. Simmer, covered, for 20 to 25 minutes, until chicken is no longer pink.

2 Meanwhile, for topping, tear bread in small pieces. Finely chop remaining celery and onion. In a small bowl toss together the bread, celery, and onion; set aside.

3 Using a slotted spoon, transfer chicken to a cutting board to cool slightly. Add noodles to simmering broth in Dutch oven; boil gently for 7 to 8 minutes, just until tender, stirring occasionally. With a slotted spoon transfer noodles, celery, and onion to a 3-quart baking dish.

4 For sauce, in a bowl whisk together sour cream, flour, and garlic powder. Gradually whisk in 1 cup of the hot broth until smooth. Add sour cream mixture to broth in Dutch oven; cook and stir until boiling.

5 Meanwhile, remove chicken from bones; discard bones. Chop chicken and add to noodles in baking dish. Gently stir in sauce. Sprinkle with bread topping, then lightly coat with cooking spray.

6 Bake, uncovered, for 30 to 35 minutes or until casserole is heated through and topping begins to brown. Sprinkle with parsley.

PER SERVING 288 **CAL**; 9 g **FAT** (3 g **SAT**); 98 mg **CHOL**; 340 mg **SODIUM**; 33 g **CARB**; 2 g **FIBER**; 19 g **PRO**

VEGETABLE-LOADED
PASTA BAKE

Vegetable-Loaded Pasta Bake

Be sure to remove the center rib of the kale before tearing the leaves. It's tough and fibrous and not particularly pleasant to eat.

MAKES 6 servings **PREP** 40 minutes
BAKE 40 minutes at 350°F

8	ounces dried whole wheat penne pasta (2¾ cups)
2½	cups cauliflower florets (half medium head)
½	cup chopped onion (1 medium)
2	cloves garlic, minced
1	tablespoon olive oil
1	cup sliced carrots (2 medium)
½	cup chopped celery (1 stalk)
12	ounces fresh kale, stems and ribs removed, leaves torn (12 cups)
½	cup frozen peas
½	cup frozen whole kernel corn
2	tablespoons butter
2	tablespoons all-purpose flour
¼	teaspoon salt
¼	teaspoon black pepper
1	cup fat-free milk
1	cup shredded extra-sharp cheddar cheese (4 ounces)
2	tablespoons finely shredded or grated Parmesan cheese

1 Preheat oven to 350°F. In a large Dutch oven cook pasta according to package directions, except add cauliflower for the last 4 minutes of cooking. Drain; rinse. Set aside.

2 In the same Dutch oven cook onion and garlic in hot oil over medium heat for 2 minutes. Add carrots and celery; cook just until carrots are tender. Add kale; cook just until wilted. Stir in pasta mixture, peas, and corn.

3 For cheese sauce, in a small saucepan melt butter; stir in flour, salt, and pepper. Add milk all at once; cook and stir until thickened and bubbly. Reduce heat; add cheddar cheese. Cook and stir until melted. Stir sauce into pasta and vegetables. Transfer to a 2½-quart casserole. Bake, covered, for 35 minutes. Sprinkle with Parmesan. Bake, uncovered, for 5 minutes more.

PER SERVING 365 **CAL**; 14 g **FAT** (7 g **SAT**); 32 mg **CHOL**; 355 mg **SODIUM**; 47 g **CARB**; 4 g **FIBER**; 15 g **PRO**

Asparagus-Tuna Casserole

Canned tuna packed in roasted-garlic olive oil infuses this casserole with fabulous flavor.

MAKES 6 servings **PREP** 20 minutes
COOK 20 minutes **BAKE** 25 minutes at 375°F

1	cup dried penne pasta
1	pound tiny new potatoes, diced (½-inch pieces)
3	tablespoons butter, melted
¼	cup chopped onion
2	tablespoons all-purpose flour
⅛	teaspoon salt
⅛	teaspoon black pepper
2¼	cups milk
2	teaspoons finely shredded lemon peel
4	ounces provolone cheese, shredded
3	4.5-ounce cans tuna packed in roasted garlic olive oil other flavor tuna*
½	cup pitted kalamata olives, halved
1½	pounds green, white, and/or purple asparagus, trimmed, cut in 1-inch pieces
¼	cup soft bread crumbs
¼	cup finely shredded Parmesan cheese

1 Preheat oven to 375°F. In a large saucepan cook pasta according to package directions, adding diced potatoes during the last 4 minutes of cooking time. Drain; set aside.

2 Meanwhile, for sauce, in a large Dutch oven cook onion in 2 tablespoons of the melted butter for 3 minutes or until tender. Stir in flour, salt, and pepper. Cook and stir 2 minutes more. Whisk in milk all at once. Add lemon peel. Cook and stir until thickened and bubbly. Whisk in provolone cheese until melted. Gently fold pasta, potatoes, tuna, olives, and asparagus into sauce. Pour into a 3-quart rectangular baking dish.

3 For topping, in a small bowl add the remaining 1 tablespoon butter. Stir in bread crumbs and Parmesan. Sprinkle on casserole. Bake, uncovered, for 25 to 30 minutes, until heated through and topping is golden.

***Tip** If tuna packed in garlic olive oil is not available, substitute tuna packed in oil and add 2 cloves of minced garlic when cooking.

PER SERVING 467 **CAL**; 21 g **FAT** (10 g **SAT**); 50 mg **CHOL**; 753 mg **SODIUM**; 36 g **CARB**; 5 g **FIBER**; 34 g **PRO**

Asian Slaw with Curried Orange Dressing

Some version of this incredibly popular noodle salad is present at most potlucks. This one is particularly pretty and packed with veggies, including napa cabbage, bok choy, snow peas, carrots, and sweet peppers.

MAKES 15 servings **START TO FINISH** 40 minutes

3	tablespoons toasted sesame oil
2	3-ounce packages ramen noodles (any flavor), broken into small pieces (discard seasoning packets or save for later use)
⅔	cup slivered almonds
8	cups shredded napa cabbage (1 large head)
3	cups shredded bok choy (1 head)
2	cups snow pea pods, trimmed and cut lengthwise into slivers (4 ounces)
2	carrots, peeled and cut into thin bite-size strips
1	red sweet pepper, cut into thin bite-size strips
¾	cup thinly sliced green onions (6)
1	cup light mayonnaise
¼	cup frozen orange juice concentrate, thawed
1	tablespoon curry powder
1	tablespoon Dijon mustard
2	cloves garlic, minced
¼	teaspoon salt
¼	teaspoon cayenne pepper

1 In a large skillet heat oil over medium-high heat. Add ramen noodles and almonds; cook and stir for 5 to 6 minutes until noodles and almonds are lightly toasted. Transfer to a baking sheet to cool.

2 In a very large bowl combine napa cabbage, bok choy, pea pods, carrots, red sweet pepper, and green onions.

3 In an extra-large bowl combine mayonnaise, orange juice concentrate, curry powder, mustard, garlic, salt, and cayenne. Whisk to a smooth dressing.

4 Just before serving, add noodle mixture and dressing to cabbage mixture; toss well to combine.

PER SERVING 189 **CAL**; 12 g **FAT** (2 g **SAT**); 6 mg **CHOL**; 240 mg **SODIUM**; 16 g **CARB**; 3 g **FIBER**; 4 g **PRO**

Potato-Cauliflower Salad

This picnic-perfect salad, featuring fingerling potatoes, cauliflower, bacon, and blue cheese is a delicious change of pace from the usual potato salad.

MAKES 8 servings **PREP** 35 minutes **CHILL** 1 hour

12	small fingerling or round new potatoes, scrubbed
1	medium head cauliflower, cut into bite-size pieces
2	tablespoons water
1	small onion, chopped
2	stalks celery, sliced
⅓	cup sour cream and chives dip
2	tablespoons lemon juice
2	tablespoons salad oil
¼	to ⅓ cup blue cheese
¼	cup chopped fresh parsley
2	slices bacon, crisp-cooked and crumbled
4	crisp breadsticks, broken
	Sea salt or salt
	Freshly ground black pepper

1 Arrange potatoes in a single layer on clean white paper towels in the microwave. Cook on high for 5 minutes. Turn potatoes; cook on high about 3 minutes more or until tender.

2 Place cauliflower and the water in a 1½-quart microwave-safe casserole. Cook on high for 5 minutes or until crisp-tender, stirring once. Drain. Cool slightly.

3 In a large serving bowl combine potatoes, cauliflower, onion, and celery. In a small bowl stir together dip, lemon juice, and salad oil; gently toss with potato mixture and fold in blue cheese. Chill for 1 to 24 hours. Just before serving, top with parsley, bacon, breadsticks, sea salt, and pepper.

PER SERVING 152 **CAL**; 7 g **FAT** (2 g **SAT**); 12 mg **CHOL**; 299 mg **SODIUM**; 18 g **CARB**; 3 g **FIBER**; 5 g **PRO**

POTATO-CAULIFLOWER SALAD

Fiesta Corn Salad

Sweet corn, edamame, and spicy jalapeños (and tomatoes, if you like) dressed in a cumin-lime dressing make a great accompaniment to grilled steak.

MAKES 12 servings **START TO FINISH** 35 minutes

4	cups fresh or frozen whole kernel corn
1	cup frozen shelled edamame, thawed
¼	cup chopped red onion
¼	cup snipped fresh cilantro
1	small fresh jalapeño, seeded and finely chopped (see tip, page 10)
2	tablespoons olive oil
½	teaspoon finely shredded lime peel
2	tablespoons lime juice
1½	teaspoons cumin seeds, toasted (see tip, page 25)
2	cloves garlic, minced
¼	teaspoon chili powder
2	medium tomatoes, seeded and chopped (optional)
	Fresh cilantro (optional)

1 In a large covered saucepan cook corn and edamame in enough boiling water to cover for 2 minutes; drain. Rinse with cold water and drain again.

2 In a large bowl stir together corn, edamame, red onion, snipped cilantro, and jalapeño.

3 For the vinaigrette, in a screw-top jar combine olive oil, lime peel and juice, cumin seeds, garlic, and chili powder. Cover and shake well.

4 Pour vinaigrette over salad, tossing gently to coat. Gently stir in tomatoes. If desired, garnish with additional cilantro. Serve immediately. (Or do not stir in tomatoes. Cover and chill in the refrigerator for up to 24 hours. Gently stir in tomatoes. Let stand for 30 minutes before serving.)

PER SERVING 96 **CAL**; 4 g **FAT** (0 g **SAT** fat), 0 g **CHOL**; 6 mg **SODIUM**; 15 g **CARB**; 2 g **FIBER**; 4 g **PRO**

Sweet and Tangy Four-Bean Salad

With edamame, wax beans, red kidney beans, and fresh green beans, this salad does the ever-popular three-bean salad one better!

MAKES 12 servings **PREP** 30 minutes **CHILL** 4 hours

8	**ounces fresh green beans, trimmed and halved or quartered**
¾	**cup cider vinegar**
⅔	**cup tomato juice**
¼	**cup vegetable oil**
3	**tablespoons dry red wine or apple juice**
½	**cup sugar**
2	**teaspoons Worcestershire sauce**
2	**teaspoons Dijon mustard**
1	**clove garlic, minced**
1	**12-ounce frozen shelled edamame, thawed**
1	**14.5-ounce can cut wax beans, rinsed and drained**
1	**15-ounce can red kidney beans, rinsed and drained**
1	**bunch green onions, finely chopped**
4	**large carrots, coarsely chopped**
	Green onion strips

1 In a large saucepan cook green beans in boiling lightly salted water for 10 minutes or just until tender; drain and rinse with cold water. Set aside.

2 In an extra-large bowl combine vinegar, tomato juice, oil, wine, sugar, Worcestershire, mustard, and garlic. Stir in edamame, wax beans, kidney beans, green onions, and carrots. Refrigerate, covered, 4 to 48 hours. Serve with a slotted spoon. To serve, top with green onion strips.

PER SERVING 174 **CAL**; 6 g **FAT** (1 g **SAT** fat); 0 g **CHOL**; 231 mg **SODIUM**; 24 g **CARB**; 6 g **FIBER**; 7 g **PRO**

Watermelon Salad

Made with fresh watermelon juice and unflavored gelatin, this shimmering retro-style fruit salad is cool in more ways than one.

MAKES 9 servings **PREP** 25 minutes **CHILL** 3 hours

2	**envelopes unflavored gelatin**
2	**cups watermelon juice***
1½	**cups white grape juice**
1	**teaspoon shredded lemon peel**
1½	**cups assorted chopped fruit (such as peeled peaches, nectarines, pears, and/or green grapes)**
⅓	**cup crumbled feta cheese**
	Mint leaves

1 In a medium saucepan sprinkle gelatin over watermelon juice. Let stand 5 minutes. Cook and stir until gelatin is dissolved. Stir in grape juice and lemon peel.

2 With a ladle or cup transfer half of the watermelon juice mixture to a 2-quart square dish. Cover and refrigerate about 1½ hours or until thickened to the texture of egg whites (keep remaining watermelon juice mixture at room temperature). Add fruit to jellied watermelon. Carefully spoon remaining watermelon juice over fruit mixture. Cover and refrigerate 1½ hours more or until all layers are set.

3 To serve, invert salad, cut in 9 squares, and top with feta and mint leaves.

*Tip For watermelon juice, process 6 cups cubed watermelon seeds removed (about 3½ pounds whole watermelon) in a food processor; strain to remove pulp.

PER SERVING 92 **CAL**; 1 g **FAT** (1 g **SAT**); 5 mg **CHOL**; 68 mg **SODIUM**; 18 g **CARB**; 1 g **FIBER**; 3 g **PRO**

Tuscan Polenta Bread

This fusion of American-style corn bread and Italian ingredients—pancetta, rosemary, and dried tomatoes—is best served warm from the oven.

MAKES 8 servings **PREP** 25 minutes **BAKE** 30 minutes at 375°F

1½ **cups cornmeal**
½ **cup all-purpose flour**
2 **tablespoons sugar**
1 **teaspoon baking soda**
¼ **teaspoon salt**
2 **tablespoons olive oil**
1¾ **cups half-and-half or light cream**
2 **eggs, lightly beaten**
9 **slices bacon or ¾ cup chopped pancetta, crisp-cooked and drained**
1 **8-ounce jar oil-packed dried tomatoes, drained and snipped**
1 **tablespoon chopped shallot**
1 **tablespoon snipped fresh rosemary**
  Butter, softened (optional)

1 Preheat oven to 375°F. In a medium bowl stir together cornmeal, flour, sugar, baking soda, and salt; set aside. Add 1 tablespoon of the oil to a 10-inch cast-iron skillet or a 9 x 1½-inch round baking pan. Place in oven for 5 minutes. Remove skillet or pan from oven; carefully swirl oil in pan to coat bottom and sides of pan.

2 Meanwhile, for batter, in a large bowl combine half-and-half, eggs, and remaining oil. Crumble bacon. Stir tomatoes, bacon, shallot, and rosemary into egg mixture until combined. Add cornmeal mixture all at once to egg mixture. Stir just until moistened. Pour batter into hot skillet or pan. Bake 30 to 35 minutes or until a wooden toothpick inserted near center comes out clean. Cut in wedges. Serve warm with softened butter, if desired.

PER SERVING 367 **CAL**; 18 g **FAT** (6 g **SAT**); 82 mg **CHOL**; 553 mg **SODIUM**; 46 g **CARB**; 2 g **FIBER**; 11 g **PRO**

Peach-Blueberry Egg Bread Bake

For a brunch or breakfast potluck, this Grand Prize Winner of the 2012 Eggland's Best "Your Best Recipe" contest is a sure bet. Donna Pochoday-Stelmach of Morristown, New Jersey, won $10,000 for her fusion of fresh fruit and eggs in a comforting egg bread-custard base. Everything that makes a healthful and tasty breakfast is in one dish!

MAKES 12 servings **PREP** 30 minutes **CHILL** 1 hour **BAKE** 1 hour at 350°F **STAND** 20 minutes

Nonstick cooking spray
2 **cups peaches, peeled and chopped (about 2 medium peaches)**
2 **cups blueberries, divided**
⅓ **cup packed brown sugar**
2 **tablespoons all-purpose flour**
5 **cups challah or brioche, cut into ½-inch pieces**
3 **Eggland's Best eggs, lightly beaten**
¼ **cup pure maple syrup**
2 **cups milk**
2 **tablespoons unsalted butter, melted**
1 **teaspoon vanilla**
1 **teaspoon ground cinnamon**
1 **cup peaches, peeled and thinly sliced**
2 **teaspoons granulated sugar**
1 **cup Greek-style vanilla yogurt (optional)**
½ **cup sliced almonds, toasted (see tip, page 25) (optional)**
 Pure maple syrup, warmed (optional)

1 Preheat oven to 350°F. Coat a deep-dish pie plate with nonstick cooking spray; set aside. In a large bowl combine chopped peaches, ¾ cup of the blueberries, brown sugar, and flour. Add bread pieces. Toss gently until mixed; set aside.

2 In a medium bowl combine eggs, ¼ cup maple syrup, milk, butter, vanilla, and cinnamon. Stir into the bread mixture. Pour into prepared pie plate. Cover and chill for 1 hour.

3 Spread the sliced peaches and remaining blueberries over the top of the egg bread. Sprinkle with granulated sugar. Place a foil-covered baking sheet on the bottom oven rack. Place pie plate on baking sheet. Bake for 1 to 1¼ hours or until bread has puffed and a knife inserted near the center comes out clean. Remove from oven. Let stand 20 to 30 minutes.

4 To serve, if desired top with yogurt, sprinkle with almonds, and drizzle with warmed maple syrup.

PER SERVING 180 **CAL**; 5 g **FAT** (3 g **SAT**); 64 mg **CHOL**; 77 mg **SODIUM**; 30 g **CARB**; 2 g **FIBER**; 5 g **PRO**

Banana-Coconut Coffee Cake with Macadamia Nut Streusel

Spike this moist banana-coconut cake with strong-brewed coffee for a breakfast or brunch treat—or with coffee liqueur to serve as dessert.

MAKES 18 servings **PREP** 30 minutes **BAKE** 35 minutes at 350°F **COOL** 30 minutes

3½   **cups all-purpose flour**
¾   **cup flaked coconut**
1   **tablespoon baking powder**
1   **teaspoon baking soda**
1   **teaspoon salt**
1   **cup butter, softened**
¾   **cup granulated sugar**
¾   **cup packed brown sugar**
4   **eggs**
3   **ripe bananas, mashed**
¼   **cup coffee liqueur or strong brewed coffee**
¼   **cup milk**
2   **teaspoons vanilla**
¼   **cup all-purpose flour**
¼   **cup packed brown sugar**
½   **teaspoon ground cinnamon**
¼   **cup cold butter, cut up**
½   **cup coarsely chopped macadamia nuts**
1   **recipe Powdered Sugar Drizzle**

1 Preheat oven to 350°F. Grease and flour a 3-quart rectangular baking pan; set aside. In a medium bowl stir together the 3½ cups flour, the coconut, baking powder, baking soda, and salt; set aside.

2 In an extra-large mixing bowl beat the 1 cup butter, ¾ cup granulated sugar, and ¾ cup brown sugar with an electric mixer on medium to high until light and fluffy. Scrape sides of bowl; beat for 1 minute. Add eggs, one at a time, beating well after each addition. Beat in bananas, liqueur, milk, and vanilla on low just until combined (mixture may appear curdled). Add flour mixture, beating on low just until combined. Spoon batter into the prepared pan, spreading evenly.

3 For streusel, in a small bowl stir together the ¼ cup flour, ¼ cup brown sugar, and the cinnamon. Using a pastry blender, cut in the ¼ cup cold butter until mixture resembles coarse crumbs. Stir in macadamia nuts. Sprinkle evenly over top of batter.

4 Bake for 35 to 40 minutes or until a wooden toothpick inserted in the center comes out clean. Cool in pan on a wire rack for 30 minutes. Drizzle with Powdered Sugar Drizzle. Serve warm.

Powdered Sugar Drizzle In a small bowl stir together ¾ cup powdered sugar, 4 teaspoons milk, ½ teaspoon vanilla, and, if desired, a few drops coconut extract until smooth.

PER SERVING 305 **CAL**; 14 g **FAT** (8 g **SAT**); 57 mg **CHOL**; 306 mg **SODIUM**; 41 g **CARB**; 1 g **FIBER**; 4 g **PRO**

handheld favorites

Forget the knives and forks—this collection of recipes requires only napkins.

MOZZARELLA-STUFFED BURGERS

BURGERS, SANDWICHES, AND WRAPS

Garlic-Mustard Steak Sandwiches

Serve this hearty bistro-style sandwich with a vinaigrette-dressed green salad and a cold beer.

MAKES 4 servings **PREP** 25 minutes **GRILL** 20 minutes

1	tablespoon honey mustard
2	cloves garlic, minced
½	teaspoon dried marjoram or thyme, crushed
¼	teaspoon coarsely ground black pepper
12	ounces beef flank steak
8	¾-ounce slices French bread
1	large red onion, cut into ½-inch-thick slices
2	tablespoons fat-free or light sour cream
2	ounces thinly sliced reduced-fat Swiss cheese

1 In a small bowl stir together honey mustard, garlic, marjoram, and pepper; set aside.

2 Trim fat from the steak. Score both sides of steak in a diamond pattern by making shallow diagonal cuts at 1-inch intervals. Spoon half of the mustard mixture onto steak; spread evenly.

3 For a charcoal or gas grill, place steak and onion slices on a grill rack directly over medium heat. Cover and grill for 17 to 21 minutes or until steak is medium doneness (160°F) and onion is tender, turning steak and onion slices once halfway through grilling. Add bread directly to the grill rack. Cover and grill for 2 to 4 minutes or until toasted, turning once halfway through grilling.

4 For sauce, in a small bowl stir together sour cream and the remaining mustard mixture. Spread on one side of half the toasted bread; set aside. Transfer steak to a cutting board; thinly slice steak across the grain. Separate onion slices into rings. Arrange steak strips, onion rings, and cheese on the toast spread with the sauce. Top with toasted bread.

PER SERVING 327 **CAL**; 9 g **FAT** (4 g **SAT**); 63 mg **CHOL**; 400 mg **SODIUM**; 33 g **CARB**; 2 g **FIBER**; 29 g **PRO**

Pepper-Steak Quesadillas

Marinating time for the steak ranges from 30 minutes to 4 hours. You'll have some flexibility in working this recipe into your busy schedule.

MAKES 4 servings **PREP** 30 minutes **MARINATE** 30 minutes **COOK** 6 minutes

8 ounces beef sirloin steak or boneless beef top round steak
1 teaspoon finely shredded lime peel
2 cloves garlic, minced
¼ teaspoon ground cumin
4 7- to 8-inch whole wheat tortillas
   Nonstick cooking spray
1 medium red sweet pepper, cut into thin bite-size strips
¼ cup thinly sliced green onions
½ cup chopped peeled jicama
½ cup reduced-fat Monterey Jack cheese, shredded (2 ounces)
   Purchased refrigerated salsa and/or lime wedges (optional)

1 Trim fat from beef. Thinly slice beef across the grain into bite-size strips.* In a medium bowl combine steak strips, lime peel, garlic, and cumin. Cover and marinate in the refrigerator for 30 minutes to 4 hours.

2 Preheat oven to 300°F. Lightly coat one side of each tortilla with cooking spray. Place tortillas, coated sides down, on a tray or clean work surface. Set aside. Coat an extra-large unheated nonstick skillet with cooking spray. Preheat skillet over medium heat. Add steak strips, sweet pepper, and green onions to hot skillet. Cook for 3 to 5 minutes or until steak is browned and pepper is crisp-tender, stirring occasionally. Remove from heat. Stir in jicama.

3 To assemble, divide steak and pepper mixture among tortillas, placing the mixture on one-half of each tortilla. Sprinkle with cheese. Fold tortillas over filling; press down lightly.

4 Coat a clean, unheated extra-large nonstick skillet or griddle with cooking spray. Preheat skillet or griddle over medium-high heat; reduce heat to medium. Cook quesadillas, half at a time, in hot skillet or griddle about 3 minutes or until tortillas are browned, turning once halfway through cooking. Place quesadillas on a baking sheet; keep warm in the oven while cooking the remaining quesadillas.

5 Cut each quesadilla into three wedges. If desired, serve with salsa and/or lime wedges.

*Tip For easy slicing, wrap and freeze steak for 30 to 45 minutes before cutting it.

PER SERVING 267 **CAL**; 9 g **FAT** (4 g **SAT**); 34 mg **CHOL**; 475 mg **SODIUM**; 20 g **CARB**; 11 g **FIBER**; 25 g **PRO**

Pork Tenderloin Sandwich with Chimichurri Sauce

Chimichurri sauce comes from Argentina, where it is as common as ketchup in this country. There it is primarily served with grilled steak, but is a wonderful all-purpose condiment for all kinds of meats, poultry, and fish.

MAKES 4 servings **PREP** 25 minutes **COOK** 5 minutes

1	cup packed fresh parsley
2	tablespoons snipped fresh oregano
2	tablespoons finely chopped shallot
2	tablespoons red wine vinegar
2	tablespoons lime juice
1	tablespoon olive oil
3	cloves garlic, minced
½	teaspoon crushed red pepper
1	pound pork tenderloin, trimmed
¼	teaspoon salt
¼	teaspoon black pepper
2	teaspoons olive oil
4	leaves lettuce
8	slices whole-grain bread, toasted
8	slices tomato

1 For Chimichurri Sauce, in a food processor or blender combine the parsley, oregano, shallot, vinegar, lime juice, 1 tablespoon olive oil, the garlic, and crushed red pepper. Cover and blend or process until finely chopped, scraping sides of bowl as necessary; set aside.

2 Cut tenderloin into 4 equal pieces. Place each piece between two pieces of plastic wrap. Using the flat side of a meat mallet, lightly pound the tenderloin to about ¼-inch thickness. Remove plastic wrap. Sprinkle evenly with salt and pepper.

3 In an extra-large nonstick skillet heat the 2 teaspoons olive oil over medium-high heat. Reduce heat to medium. Cook tenderloin in hot oil for 5 to 7 minutes or until just pink inside. Remove from heat.

4 To assemble sandwiches, place a lettuce leaf on each of 4 slices toast. Top with tenderloin, some of the Chimichurri Sauce, tomato slices, and toast slice.

PER SERVING 343 **CAL**; 10 g **FAT** (2 g **SAT**); 70 mg **CHOL**; 506 mg **SODIUM**; 30 g **CARB**; 6 g **FIBER**; 32 g **PRO**

Mozzarella-Stuffed Burgers

These indulgent cheese-stuffed burgers, made with ground beef and Italian sausage then topped with Basil-Olive Mayonnaise, are well worth the occasional indiscretion.

MAKES 6 servings **PREP** 30 minutes **GRILL** 20 minutes

¾   **cup freshly grated Parmesan cheese**
½   **cup snipped fresh basil (optional)**
⅓   **cup snipped oil-packed dried tomatoes, drained**
3   **cloves garlic, minced**
½   **teaspoon freshly ground black pepper**
¼   **teaspoon salt**
1½ **pounds 85% lean ground beef**
8   **ounces bulk Italian sausage**
6   **ounces fresh mozzarella cheese**
1   **recipe Basil-Olive Mayonnaise**
6   **hamburger buns or ciabatta rolls, split**
    Basil leaves (optional)

1 In a large bowl combine Parmesan cheese, basil (if using), tomatoes, garlic, pepper, and salt. Add ground beef and Italian sausage; mix well. Shape meat mixture into twelve ½-inch-thick patties.

2 Cut mozzarella cheese into six ¼-inch-thick slices. Place mozzarella cheese on the centers of 6 of the patties. Top with the remaining 6 patties; pinch edges together to seal.

3 For a charcoal grill, arrange medium-hot coals around a drip pan. Test for medium heat above pan. Place patties on grill rack over drip pan. Cover and grill for 20 to 25 minutes or until done (160°F), turning patties once halfway through grilling. (For a gas grill, preheat grill. Reduce heat to medium. Adjust for indirect cooking and grill as above.)

4 Spread Basil-Olive Mayonnaise on bottoms of buns. Top with basil leaves, if desired, then patties and bun tops.

Basil-Olive Mayonnaise In a small bowl combine ⅓ cup mayonnaise, 1 tablespoon kalamata olive tapenade, and 1 tablespoon snipped fresh basil.

PER SERVING 734 **CAL**; 50 g **FAT** (19 g **SAT**); 141 mg **CHOL**; 1,025 mg **SODIUM**; 29 g **CARB**; 1 g **FIBER**; 41 g **PRO**

Skillet Chicken Salad Pitas

A sweet and spicy Asian-style marinade flavors chunks of chicken breast dressed with a cilantro-lime mayo then tucked into pita bread with crunchy lettuce.

MAKES 8 servings **PREP** 30 minutes **MARINATE** 1 hour
CHILL 1 hour **COOK** 11 minutes

- ⅓ **cup snipped fresh cilantro**
- ¼ **cup Asian sweet chili sauce**
- 4 **tablespoons lime juice**
- 1 **tablespoon minced garlic**
- 1 **teaspoon olive oil**
- ⅛ **teaspoon kosher salt or salt**
- 2 **pounds skinless, boneless chicken breast halves, cut into 1-inch pieces**
- 1 **large red sweet pepper, cut into bite-size strips**
- ⅔ **cup mayonnaise**
- ½ **cup snipped fresh cilantro**
- 8 **pita bread rounds**
- 8 **leaves red or green leaf lettuce**

1 For marinade, combine the ⅓ cup cilantro, chili sauce, 2 tablespoons of the lime juice, garlic, oil, and salt in a resealable plastic bag set in shallow dish. Add chicken. Seal bag and turn to coat. Marinate in the refrigerator 1 hour. Drain chicken from bag; discard marinade.

2 Heat an extra-large skillet over medium-high heat. Add chicken, half at a time, and cook 3 minutes per batch, stirring occasionally. Return all chicken to skillet. Add sweet pepper; cook for 5 minutes or until chicken is no longer pink, stirring occasionally. Using a slotted spoon transfer chicken salad to large bowl. Cover; refrigerate 1 to 8 hours.

3 For dressing, in a bowl combine mayonnaise, the ½ cup cilantro, and remaining lime juice. To serve, top each pita with a lettuce leaf. Spoon chicken salad on half of each pita (if necessary, drain excess liquid from chicken). Drizzle with dressing.

PER SERVING 456 **CAL**; 18 g **FAT** (3 g **SAT**); 73 mg **CHOL**; 644 mg **SODIUM**; 38 g **CARB**; 2 g **FIBER**; 33 g **PRO**

Chicken and Black Bean Pesto Wraps

The black bean spread can be made up to a day ahead, then covered and refrigerated until ready to use. For spreading, it can be slightly warmed in a microwave.

MAKES 4 servings **PREP** 20 minutes **COOK** 4 minutes

- 1 **15-ounce can no-salt-added black beans, rinsed and drained**
- ½ **cup loosely packed cilantro leaves**
- ¼ **cup chopped onion**
- 3 **tablespoons lime juice**
- 1 **teaspoon chili powder**
- 2 **cloves garlic, minced**
- ¼ **teaspoon crushed red pepper**
- ¼ **teaspoon salt**
- 12 **ounces skinless, boneless chicken breast halves, cut into strips**
- ½ **teaspoon dried oregano, crushed**
- 2 **teaspoons olive oil**
- 4 **multigrain flatbread wraps**
- 2 **cups shredded fresh spinach**
- 1 **small red sweet pepper, cut into bite-size strips**

1 In a medium bowl combine beans, cilantro, onion, 1 tablespoon of the lime juice, ½ teaspoon of the chili powder, the garlic, crushed red pepper, and ⅛ teaspoon of the salt. Mash with a potato masher until almost smooth. Set aside.

2 In a medium bowl toss chicken breast strips with the remaining chili powder, oregano, and remaining salt to coat. In a large nonstick skillet cook chicken in hot oil over medium-high heat for 4 to 5 minutes or until chicken is no longer pink. Remove from heat and stir in the remaining 2 tablespoons lime juice.

3 To assemble wraps, spread bean mixture evenly on wraps. Top with spinach, sweet pepper strips, and chicken, then roll around filling.

PER SERVING 311 **CAL**; 7 g **FAT** (1 g **SAT**); 54 mg **CHOL**; 561 mg **SODIUM**; 35 g **CARB**; 14 g **FIBER**; 33 g **PRO**

Spicy Turkey Cranberry Grilled Cheese

With two kinds of cheese, butter, and bacon, you know this sandwich—slathered with spicy cranberry jalapeño jelly—is a winner. That's what the judges of the 2013 Tillamook Cheese Factory Grilled Cheese contest thought too. Karla Pollich of Portland, Oregon, walked away with the 1st-place prize of $500, a gift basket chock-full of Tillamook goodies, and the honor of having her sandwich featured at the Tillamook Creamery Café for the week following the contest. Read more of Karla's foodie thoughts at her blog, cookingwithkarla.wordpress.com.

MAKES 2 servings **PREP** 10 minutes **COOK** 6 minutes

4	slices sourdough bread
4	slices Tillamook Swiss cheese
4	slices thick-cut bacon, crisp-cooked
4	large slices herb-roasted turkey
3	tablespoons Wildtree cranberry jalapeño jelly*
2	¼-inch-thick slices Tillamook Vintage white-extra sharp cheddar cheese
4	tablespoons Tillamook unsalted butter, softened

1 Place 2 slices of bread on a work surface. Top each slice with 2 slices Swiss cheese, 2 slices bacon, and 2 slices turkey. Spread 1½ tablespoons cranberry jelly over turkey; top with 1 slice white cheddar cheese. Top with another slice of bread; spread bread with half of the butter. Place sandwich, buttered slice down, in a skillet over medium heat. Carefully spread unbuttered bread slices with remaining butter.

2 Cook sandwiches for 3 minutes per side or until bread is golden and cheese is melted. Slice in half to serve.

***Tip** If you are not able to locate this product, in a small bowl combine 2 tablespoons red or green jalapeño jelly, 1 tablespoon canned whole cranberry sauce, and ⅛ teaspoon dried mint or ¼ teaspoon snipped fresh mint.

PER SERVING 1,137 **CAL**; 65 g **FAT** (36 g **SAT**); 392 mg **CHOL**; 1,103 mg **SODIUM**; 54 g **CARB**; 2 g **FIBER**; 83 g **PRO**

Greek Salad Club

For a little something different, the pita breads are split open (so you have two thin rounds of bread) then toasted before filling with hummus, cheese, and veggies.

MAKES 4 servings **START TO FINISH** 25 minutes

6	flat pita bread rounds, opened to halves and toasted
1	7-ounce container purchased hummus
4	romaine lettuce leaves
1	large tomato, sliced
1	yellow sweet pepper, seeded and sliced
½	English cucumber, sliced
2	ounces feta cheese, crumbled
¼	cup lightly packed fresh oregano leaves
¼	cup purchased Greek vinaigrette dressing

1 Spread 8 pita halves with hummus. Layer 4 of the spread slices with romaine, tomato, and sweet pepper slices. Top with 4 spread pita halves, hummus side up. Layer cucumber, feta cheese, and fresh oregano. Drizzle with dressing. Top with remaining 4 pita halves.

PER SERVING 454 **CAL**; 14 g **FAT** (4 g **SAT**); 13 mg **CHOL**; 975 mg **SODIUM**; 66 g **CARB**; 7 g **FIBER**; 16 g **PRO**

Spinach Fontina Stromboli

Frozen whole wheat bread dough gives you a jump-start on making this stuffed and spiraled Italian sandwich.

MAKES 4 servings **PREP** 20 minutes **RISE** 20 minutes **BAKE** 25 minutes at 375°F **STAND** 10 minutes

2	teaspoons olive oil
1	tablespoon cornmeal
1	16-ounce loaf frozen whole wheat bread dough, thawed
1	cup shredded fontina cheese (4 ounces)
1	cup baby spinach or torn spinach
¼	cup kalamata olives, pitted and chopped
1	egg, lightly beaten

1 Lightly brush a baking sheet with olive oil; sprinkle with cornmeal. Set aside. On a lightly floured surface, roll bread dough into a 13 x 10-inch rectangle. Sprinkle with half the cheese. Layer spinach over cheese. Top with remaining cheese and olives. Roll up dough, starting from the long side. Pinch dough to seal the seam and ends, using wet fingers, if necessary.

2 Place loaf, seam side down, on prepared baking sheet. Brush with egg. Using a sharp knife, cut slits in the top for steam to escape. Cover and let rise in a warm place for 20 to 25 minutes.

3 Preheat oven to 375°F. Bake for 25 minutes or until golden brown. Let stand 10 minutes. Slice to serve.

PER SERVING 506 **CAL**; 22 g **FAT** (7 g **SAT**); 79 mg **CHOL**; 665 mg **SODIUM**; 61 g **CARB**; 6 g **FIBER**; 19 g **PRO**

Banana-Nut Pound Cake

A whole tablespoon of vanilla and a spike of bourbon give this pecan-studded cake amazing flavor.

MAKES 12 servings **STAND** 30 minutes **PREP** 25 minutes **BAKE** 1 hour 10 minutes at 325°F **COOL** 15 minutes

1	**8-ounce package cream cheese, softened**
½	**cup butter, softened**
4	**eggs**
3¼	**cups all-purpose flour**
½	**teaspoon baking powder**
½	**teaspoon salt**
3	**cups granulated sugar**
1	**cup mashed bananas (3 medium)**
¼	**cup bourbon or low-fat milk**
1	**tablespoon vanilla**
1	**cup chopped pecans, toasted (see tip, page 25)**
	Powdered sugar
	Fresh berries (optional)

1 Allow cream cheese, butter, and eggs to stand at room temperature for 30 minutes. Meanwhile, grease and flour a 10-inch fluted tube pan; set aside. In a large bowl combine flour, baking powder, and salt; set aside.

2 Preheat oven to 325°F. In a large mixing bowl beat cream cheese and butter with an electric mixer on medium until combined. Gradually add granulated sugar, beating about 7 minutes or until light and fluffy. Add eggs, one at a time, beating well after each addition. In a bowl combine mashed bananas, bourbon, and vanilla. Alternately add flour mixture and banana mixture to butter mixture, beat on low to medium after each addition just until combined. Stir in pecans. Pour batter into the prepared pan, spreading evenly (pan will be full).

3 Bake for 70 to 85 minutes or until a toothpick inserted near the center comes out clean. Cool cake in pan on a wire rack for 15 minutes. Remove from pan; cool on rack. Sprinkle with powdered sugar. If desired, serve with berries.

PER SERVING 573 **CAL**; 23 g **FAT** (10 g **SAT**); 103 mg **CHOL**; 271 mg **SODIUM**; 84 g **CARB**; 2 g **FIBER**; 8 g **PRO**

Vanilla Cake with Buttercream, Berries, and Jam

This ethereal cake perfectly vehicle for showcases ripe and juicy summer berries.

MAKES 12 servings **PREP** 40 minutes **BAKE** 22 minutes at 350°F **COOL** 10 minutes **STAND** 30 minutes

4	egg whites
2½	cups all-purpose flour
⅓	cup cornstarch
3½	teaspoons baking powder
1	teaspoon salt
¾	cup water
⅔	cup vegetable oil
½	cup milk
1	tablespoon vanilla
¼	teaspoon cream of tartar
1½	cups sugar
½	cup butter
6	cups powdered sugar
3	tablespoons milk
2	teaspoons vanilla or vanilla bean paste
	Milk (optional)
1	cup strawberry jam
3	cups sliced fresh strawberries, raspberries, blackberries, and/or blueberries, stemmed and halved
1	cup whole fresh strawberries, raspberries, blackberries, and/or blueberries

1 Allow egg whites to stand at room temperature for 30 minutes. Grease bottoms of two 8 x 1½-inch round cake pans. Line bottoms with parchment paper or waxed paper; grease and lightly flour pans. Set pans aside.

2 Preheat oven to 350°F. In a large bowl stir together flour, cornstarch, baking powder, and salt. Add the water, oil, milk, and vanilla. Beat with a wire whisk until smooth.

3 In a medium mixing bowl combine egg whites and cream of tartar. Beat with an electric mixer on medium until soft peaks form (tips curl). Gradually add sugar, beating on high until stiff peaks form (tips stand straight). Fold beaten egg whites into batter. Pour batter into prepared pans, spreading evenly.

4 Bake for 22 to 25 minutes or until a toothpick inserted near centers comes out clean. Cool in pans on wire racks for 10 minutes. Remove from pans; cool thoroughly on wire racks.

5 Meanwhile, for the vanilla-butter frosting, allow butter to stand at room temperature for 30 minutes. In a medium mixing bowl beat butter with an electric mixer on medium to high for 30 seconds. Gradually add 3 cups of the powdered sugar, beating well. Beat in the 3 tablespoons milk and the vanilla. Gradually beat in the remaining 3 cups powdered sugar. If necessary, beat in additional milk, 1 teaspoon at a time, to make spreading consistency.

6 To assemble, use a long serrated knife to cut cake layers in half horizontally. Place one cake layer, cut side down, on a serving plate. Spread with a generous ¾ cup of the frosting and ¼ cup of the jam. Top with 1 cup of the sliced berries. Repeat with two more cake layers.

7 For top layer, add final cake layer cut side down. Spread with ¾ cup frosting, ¼ cup jam, and top with the 1 cup whole berries.

PER SERVING 722 **CAL**; 20 g **FAT** (6 g **SAT**); 21 mg **CHOL**; 404 mg **SODIUM**; 132 g **CARB**; 2 g **FIBER**; 5 g **PRO**

Sticky Pecan Upside-Down Baby Cakes

These sour-cream cakes have the fabulous ooey-gooeyness of sticky buns without the rising time, rolling, and shaping required by yeast breads.

MAKES 12 servings **PREP** 20 minutes **BAKE** 25 minutes at 350°F **COOL** 5 minutes

Nonstick cooking spray
2½ cups all-purpose flour
1 teaspoon baking powder
½ teaspoon baking soda
½ teaspoon salt
⅔ cup packed brown sugar
½ cup butter
⅓ cup honey
1½ cups coarsely chopped pecans
1 teaspoon finely shredded orange peel
3 eggs
2 cups granulated sugar
1 cup vegetable oil
1 8-ounce carton sour cream
2 teaspoons vanilla
Caramel sauce (optional)

1 Preheat oven to 350°F. Lightly coat twelve 3½-inch (jumbo) muffin cups with cooking spray; set aside. In a medium bowl stir together flour, baking powder, baking soda, and salt; set aside.

2 In a medium saucepan combine brown sugar, butter, and honey. Cook and stir over medium heat for 2 minutes or until smooth; remove from heat. Stir in pecans and orange peel; set aside.

3 In a large mixing bowl combine eggs and granulated sugar. Beat with an electric mixer on medium to high for 3 minutes or until mixture is thick and lemon color. Add oil, sour cream, and vanilla; beat until combined. Gradually add flour mixture, beating on low until smooth.

4 Place 2 tablespoons of the pecan mixture in the bottom of each muffin cup. Spoon a heaping ⅓ cup of the batter into each cup. Place muffin pans on a large foil-lined baking sheet.

5 Bake for 25 to 30 minutes or until a wooden toothpick inserted in the centers comes out clean. Cool cakes in pans on a wire rack for 5 minutes. Using a sharp knife or thin spatula, loosen cakes from sides of muffin cups. Invert onto wire rack. Spoon any pecan topping remaining in the muffin cups onto cakes. Serve warm or cool. If desired, serve with caramel sauce.

PER SERVING 679 **CAL**; 41 g **FAT** (10 g **SAT**); 83 mg **CHOL**; 271 mg **SODIUM**; 76 g **CARB**; 2 g **FIBER**; 6 g **PRO**

Hot Cocoa Soufflé with Coffee Ice Cream

Gather guests to the table before you take this high-rising chocolate dessert from the oven. It will begin to fall immediately. A scoop of coffee ice cream on the side makes it mocha.

MAKES 6 servings **STAND** 30 minutes **PREP** 25 minutes **BAKE** 40 minutes at 350°F

4	**egg yolks**
4	**egg whites**
3	**tablespoons sugar**
2	**tablespoons unsweetened Dutch-process cocoa powder**
¼	**cup butter**
½	**cup sugar**
½	**cup unsweetened Dutch-process cocoa powder**
¼	**cup all-purpose flour**
1	**cup milk**
2	**tablespoons sugar**
1	**quart coffee ice cream**

1 Allow egg yolks and egg whites to stand at room temperature for 30 minutes.

2 Meanwhile, preheat oven to 350°F. Butter the sides of a 1½-quart oven-proof mixing bowl or soufflé dish. In a small bowl stir together the 3 tablespoons sugar and the 2 tablespoons cocoa powder. Sprinkle the inside of the prepared bowl or dish with enough of the sugar-cocoa mixture to coat bottom and sides; set bowl and the remaining sugar-cocoa mixture aside.

3 In a medium saucepan heat the butter over medium heat until melted. Stir in the ½ cup sugar, the ½ cup cocoa powder, and the flour. Add milk all at once. Cook and stir until thickened and bubbly. Remove from heat. In a medium bowl beat egg yolks with a fork until combined. Gradually stir milk mixture into beaten egg yolks. Set aside.

4 In a large mixing bowl beat egg whites with an electric mixer on medium to high until soft peaks form (tips curl). Gradually add the 2 tablespoons sugar, beating until stiff peaks form (tips stand straight) and sugar is completely dissolved. Fold 1 cup of the beaten egg whites into egg yolk mixture. Fold egg yolk mixture into the remaining beaten egg whites. Transfer batter to the prepared bowl.

5 Bake for 40 to 45 minutes or until a knife inserted near the center comes out clean. Immediately sprinkle top of baked soufflé with the remaining sugar-cocoa mixture. Serve with scoops of ice cream or, if desired, place scoops of ice cream in center of soufflé to serve.

PER SERVING 484 **CAL**; 24 g **FAT** (13 g **SAT**); 178 mg **CHOL**; 206 mg **SODIUM**; 59 g **CARB**; 2 g **FIBER**; 11 g **PRO**

Maple Bread Pudding with Pecan Praline

The crunchy pecan praline candy that serves as a topping for this decadent bread pudding can be made a day or two ahead. When it is completely cool, store it at room temperature in a tightly sealed container.

MAKES 12 servings **PREP** 35 minutes **CHILL** 1 hour **BAKE** 40 minutes at 375°F **COOL** 30 minutes

1	**cup granulated sugar**
¼	**cup water**
½	**cup chopped pecans, toasted (see tip, page 25)**
8	**eggs**
4	**cups half-and-half or light cream**
1	**cup packed brown sugar**
1	**cup maple syrup**
1	**tablespoon vanilla**
1	**1-pound loaf egg bread, torn into bite-size pieces (about 14 cups)**
	Vanilla ice cream (optional)

1 For pecan praline, lightly grease a baking sheet; set aside. In a small saucepan combine granulated sugar and the water. Cook over medium heat, stirring to dissolve sugar. Bring to boiling; reduce heat. Without stirring, boil gently, uncovered, about 7 minutes or until mixture turns a deep amber color. Remove from heat. Stir in pecans. Quickly pour onto the prepared baking sheet. Cool. Break or chop into pieces; set aside.

2 In an extra-large bowl whisk together eggs, half-and-half, brown sugar, maple syrup, and vanilla. Add bread pieces; stir to moisten evenly. Cover and chill for 1 hour.

3 Preheat oven to 375°F. Lightly grease a 3-quart rectangular baking dish. Transfer bread mixture to the prepared baking dish. Bake, uncovered, about 40 minutes or until golden brown and a knife inserted in the center comes out clean. Cool on a wire rack for 30 minutes.

4 To serve, spoon warm bread pudding into bowls. If desired, top with ice cream. Sprinkle with pecan praline.

PER SERVING 647 **CAL**; 26 g **FAT** (13 g **SAT**); 222 mg **CHOL**; 331 mg **SODIUM**; 92 g **CARB**; 2 g **FIBER**; 13 g **PRO**

Almond-Cherry Cheesecake Ribbon Pie

When you can't decide between cheesecake and pie, this dessert offers the best of both worlds.

MAKES 12 servings **PREP** 45 minutes **CHILL** 1 hour + 4 hours **BAKE** 23 minutes at 425°F/25 minutes at 350°F

2	15-ounce cans pitted tart red cherries (water pack)
1	cup sugar
¼	cup cornstarch
1	cup all-purpose flour
¼	cup finely ground almonds
1	teaspoon sugar
½	teaspoon salt
6	tablespoons butter, cut up
3	to 4 tablespoons ice water
1	8-ounce package cream cheese
2	eggs
½	cup sugar
½	teaspoon vanilla
¼	teaspoon almond extract
	Toasted sliced almonds (see tip, page 25) (optional)

1 For filling, drain cherries, reserving 1 cup of the liquid. In a medium saucepan stir together the 1 cup sugar and the cornstarch. Add cherries and the reserved liquid. Bring to boiling, stirring to dissolve sugar; reduce heat. Boil gently, uncovered, for 1 minute; cool. Cover and chill until needed.

2 For pastry, in a medium bowl stir together flour, ground almonds, the 1 teaspoon sugar, and the salt. Using a pastry blender, cut in butter until pieces are pea size. Sprinkle 1 tablespoon of the water over part of the flour mixture; toss gently with a fork. Push moistened pastry to one side of bowl. Repeat moistening flour mixture, using 1 tablespoon of the water at a time, until all of the flour mixture is moistened. Gather flour mixture into a ball, kneading gently until it holds together. Cover and chill for 1 hour.

3 Meanwhile, allow cream cheese and eggs to stand at room temperature for 30 minutes. Preheat oven to 425°F. On a lightly floured surface, roll pastry into an 11-inch circle. Ease pastry circle into a 9-inch pie plate. Trim pastry to ½ inch beyond edge of pie plate. Fold under pastry edge; crimp edge as desired. Line the pastry with heavy duty foil. Bake for 8 minutes. Remove foil. Spoon half of the cherry filling into pastry-lined pie plate. Bake for 15 minutes.

4 In a large mixing bowl beat cream cheese with an electric mixer on medium to high for 30 seconds. Add the ½ cup sugar, the vanilla, and almond extract; beat until combined. Using a fork, lightly beat eggs. Add eggs to cream cheese mixture; beat just until combined.

5 Reduce oven temperature to 350°F. Spread cream cheese mixture evenly over cherry layer in pie plate. Bake for 25 minutes or until cream cheese layer is set, covering with foil if necessary to prevent crust from overbrowning. Cool on a wire rack.

6 Spread the remaining cherry filling over cream cheese layer. Cover and chill for at least 4 hours or overnight. If desired, sprinkle with sliced almonds before serving.

PER SERVING 329 **CAL**; 16 g **FAT** (9 g **SAT**); 72 mg **CHOL**; 243 mg **SODIUM**; 44 g **CARB**; 1 g **FIBER**; 4 g **PRO**

Granny Smith Cobbler with White Cheddar Biscuits

*A wedge of cheddar cheese is a traditional accompaniment to apple pie in parts of New England.
This recipe offers up that combination in a new form—tart apples topped with warm cheddary biscuits.*

MAKES 12 servings **PREP** 35 minutes **BAKE** 25 minutes at 400°F **COOL** 30 minutes

3	pounds Granny Smith apples, peeled, cored, and sliced (about 9 cups)
1	cup packed dark brown sugar
1	tablespoon balsamic vinegar
1	teaspoon ground cinnamon
¼	cup cold water
3	tablespoons cornstarch
1½	cups all-purpose flour
½	cup finely ground pecans or almonds or ½ cup all-purpose flour
3	tablespoons granulated sugar
1	tablespoon baking powder
1	teaspoon salt
½	cup butter
2	eggs, lightly beaten
½	cup milk
½	cup shredded aged white cheddar cheese (2 ounces)
	Vanilla ice cream (optional)

1 Preheat oven to 400°F. In a 4- to 6-quart Dutch oven combine apples, brown sugar, balsamic vinegar, and cinnamon. Bring to boiling, stirring occasionally once apples begin to release their juices. Reduce heat; simmer, covered, about 5 minutes or until apples are nearly tender, stirring occasionally. In a small bowl stir together the cold water and cornstarch; add to apple mixture. Cook and stir until thickened and bubbly. Keep hot over low heat.

2 In a large bowl combine flour, ground nuts, granulated sugar, baking powder, and salt. Using a pastry blender, cut in butter until pieces are pea size. In a medium bowl stir together eggs, milk, and cheese. Add cheese mixture to flour mixture; stir just until combined. Spoon hot apple mixture evenly into a 3-quart rectangular baking dish. Using a spoon, drop dough mixture into 12 mounds on top of fruit.

3 Bake for 25 to 30 minutes or until top is golden and filling is bubbly. Cool on a wire rack for 30 minutes. Serve warm. If desired, top with ice cream.

PER SERVING 326 CAL; 14 g FAT (7 g SAT); 61 mg CHOL; 390 mg SODIUM; 48 g CARB; 2 g FIBER; 5 g PRO

Peach-Mango Pie

To prepare the mango, stand it on end and cut down from top to bottom on either side of the large pit. Use a paring knife or vegetable peeler to remove the peel, then slice each piece; discard the pit.

MAKES 8 servings **PREP** 30 minutes **BAKE** 50 minutes at 375°F **COOL** 2 hours

2½   **cups all-purpose flour**
1   **teaspoon salt**
¾   **cup shortening**
½   **to ¾ cup milk**
1   **cup sugar**
2   **tablespoons all-purpose flour**
¼   **teaspoon ground ginger**
⅛   **teaspoon ground nutmeg**
¼   **teaspoon ground cinnamon**
¼   **teaspoon salt**
3   **cups thinly sliced peeled fresh peaches or frozen unsweetened peach slices, thawed**
3   **cups sliced, seeded, and peeled fresh mangoes**
2   **teaspoons fresh lime juice**
1   **egg white**
     Coarse sugar
     Vanilla ice cream (optional)

1 Preheat oven to 375°F. For the pastry, in a medium bowl combine flour and salt. Cut in shortening until pieces are pea size. Sprinkle 1 tablespoon milk over mixture; toss with a fork. Repeat, adding 1 tablespoon milk at a time, until moistened. Gather into a ball; knead gently. Divide in half. On a lightly floured surface, roll one ball into a 12-inch circle. Transfer to a 9-inch pie plate. Cover; set aside.

2 For filling, combine sugar, flour, ginger, nutmeg, cinnamon, and salt. Add fruit; toss to coat. Transfer to pastry-lined pie plate. Drizzle with lime juice. Trim pastry.

3 Roll remaining pastry into a 12-inch circle. Cut slits in pastry; place on filling. Trim to ½ inch beyond edge; fold under bottom pastry. Crimp edge. Combine egg white and 1 tablespoon water. Brush over pastry. Sprinkle with 1 teaspoon coarse sugar. Cover edge with foil. Place pie on middle oven rack with a foil-lined baking sheet on rack below.

4 Bake 25 minutes. Remove foil from pie; bake 25 minutes more or until filling is bubbly. Cool on a wire rack. Serve with vanilla ice cream if desired.

PER SERVING 489 **CAL**; 20 g **FAT** (5 g **SAT**); 1 mg **CHOL**; 380 mg **SODIUM**; 73 g **CARB**; 3 g **FIBER**; 6 g **PRO**

Dulce de Leche-Hazelnut-Pumpkin Pie

Dulce de leche, popular in Latin countries, is a creamy caramel made from sweetened milk. Look for it in the baking aisle of your supermarket.

MAKES 8 servings **PREP** 40 minutes **CHILL** 30 minutes **BAKE** 50 minutes at 350°F

1   recipe Hazelnut Pastry
1   8-ounce package cream cheese, softened
4   tablespoons dulce de leche
1   egg
1¼   cups canned pumpkin
½   cup evaporated milk
2   eggs
⅓   cup sugar
2   tablespoons hazelnut or almond liqueur
     (optional)
1½   teaspoons pumpkin pie spice
1   recipe Dulce de Leche-Hazelnut Whipped Cream
     Chopped hazelnuts (filberts), toasted* (optional)
     Dulce de leche (optional)

1 On a floured surface, roll Hazelnut Pastry into a 12-inch circle. Ease pastry circle into a 9-inch pie plate without stretching it. Trim pastry to ½ inch beyond edge of pie plate. Fold under extra pastry. Crimp edge as desired.

2 In a small mixing bowl beat cream cheese and 2 tablespoons of the dulce de leche with an electric mixer on medium to high for 30 seconds. Add 1 egg; beat on medium until smooth. Spread evenly in the pastry-lined plate. Cover and chill for 30 minutes.

3 Preheat oven to 350°F. In a medium bowl whisk together pumpkin, evaporated milk, 2 eggs, sugar, the remaining 2 tablespoons dulce de leche, the hazelnut liqueur (if desired), and pumpkin pie spice. Carefully pour pumpkin mixture over cream cheese layer.

4 Cover edge of pie loosely with foil. Bake for 25 minutes; remove foil. Bake about 25 minutes more or until filling is set in the center. Cool on a wire rack.

5 To serve, top pie with Dulce de Leche-Hazelnut Whipped Cream, sprinkle with hazelnuts (if desired), and drizzle with additional dulce de leche (if necessary, stir in a little milk to thin for drizzling).

Hazelnut Pastry In a medium bowl stir together 1 cup all-purpose flour; ¼ cup finely ground hazelnuts, almonds, or all-purpose flour; and ¼ teaspoon salt. Using a pastry blender, cut in ⅓ cup shortening until pieces are pea size. Sprinkle 1 tablespoon ice water over part of the flour mixture; toss with a fork. Push moistened pastry to one side of the bowl. Repeat moistening flour mixture, using 1 tablespoon ice water at a time, until all is moistened (4 to 5 tablespoons ice water total). Gather flour into a ball, kneading gently until it holds together.

Dulce de Leche-Hazelnut Whipped Cream Place 1 tablespoon dulce de leche in a small chilled mixing bowl. If desired, add 2 teaspoons hazelnut liqueur. Beat with the chilled beaters of an electric mixer on medium to high until smooth. Add 1 cup whipping cream. Beat on medium just until stiff peaks begin to form (tips stand straight).

*Tip To toast hazelnuts, preheat oven to 350°F. Spread nuts in a single layer in a shallow baking pan. Bake for 8 to 10 minutes or until lightly toasted, stirring once to toast evenly. Cool nuts slightly. Place the warm nuts on a clean kitchen towel; rub with the towel to remove the loose skins.

PER SERVING 496 **CAL**; 35 g **FAT** (17 g **SAT**); 152 mg **CHOL**; 243 mg **SODIUM**; 37 g **CARB**; 2 g **FIBER**; 9 g **PRO**

Sittin' on the Sandbar Key Lime Pie

English teacher Amy Freeze dreamed up the idea for the coconut-lime pie that won her $5,000 and Best in Show in the amateur division of the 2013 National Pie Championships while lounging in a chair at the water's edge in the blue-green shallows of Florida's Little Gasparilla Island. Amy tested her creation on her husband, children, and lucky students and co-workers. Unlike most key lime pies, this pie is popped briefly in the oven. When chilled, the filling sets up nicely, Amy says, resulting in "a super creamy pie that's tart and sweet but doesn't weep."

MAKES 8 servings **PREP** 1 hour **BAKE** 10 minutes at 350°F/45 minutes at 325°F **CHILL** 2 hours

2	cups crushed vanilla wafers
2	tablespoons granulated sugar
5	tablespoons melted butter
8	ounces Philadelphia cream cheese, softened
2	eggs
2	egg yolks
1	14-ounce can Eagle Brand sweetened condensed milk
¾	cup fresh squeezed Key lime juice (12 to 16 Key limes)
¾	cup Coco Lopez cream of coconut
1	cup whipping cream
1	cup powdered sugar
	Key lime slices and wedges

1 Preheat oven to 350°F. For the piecrust, in a medium bowl combine crushed vanilla wafers, sugar, and melted butter. Press into a 9-inch deep dish pie plate. Bake 10 minutes. Cool on a wire rack before filling. Reduce oven temperature to 325°F.

2 In a medium mixing bowl beat cream cheese with an electric mixer on medium for 30 seconds or until smooth. Add eggs and egg yolks, one at a time, beating well after each addition. Add sweetened condensed milk; beat well. Add key lime juice and cream of coconut; beat well. Pour into piecrust.

3 Bake for 45 minutes or until center is set. Cool completely on a wire rack. Chill for 2 to 3 hours before serving; cover for longer storage.

4 Before serving, in a large cold mixing bowl beat whipping cream and powdered sugar on medium-high until stiff peaks form (tips stand straight). Pipe large rosettes around edges of pie. Garnish with key lime slices and wedges.

PER SERVING 746 **CAL**; 43 g **FAT** (26 g **SAT**); 201 mg **CHOL**; 359 mg **SODIUM**; 82 g **CARB**; 1 g **FIBER**; 10 g **PRO**

Fudge Ripple Pecan Brownies

Pecans, caramel, and a double dose of chocolate—need we say more?

MAKES 16 servings **PREP** 30 minutes **BAKE** 30 minutes at 350°F **STAND** 2 hours

½ **cup butter**

3 **ounces unsweetened chocolate, coarsely chopped**

1 **cup sugar**

2 **eggs**

1 **teaspoon vanilla**

⅔ **cup all-purpose flour**

¼ **teaspoon baking soda**

1 **cup chopped pecans, toasted (see tip, page 25)**

¾ **cup semisweet chocolate pieces**

20 **vanilla caramels, unwrapped**

1 **tablespoon milk**

1 In a medium saucepan heat and stir butter and unsweetened chocolate over low heat until melted and smooth. Remove from heat. Set aside to cool.

2 Meanwhile, preheat oven to 350°F. Line an 8 x 8 x 2-inch baking pan with foil, extending the foil about 1 inch beyond edges of pan. Grease foil; set pan aside.

3 Stir sugar into the cooled chocolate mixture in saucepan. Add the eggs, one at a time, beating with a wooden spoon after each addition just until combined. Stir in vanilla. In a small bowl stir together the flour and baking soda. Add flour mixture to chocolate mixture, stirring just until combined. Stir in ½ cup of the pecans and ½ cup of the chocolate pieces. Spread batter evenly in the prepared pan.

4 Bake for 30 minutes. Cool in pan on a wire rack.

5 Meanwhile, in a small saucepan heat and stir unwrapped caramels and milk over medium-low heat until melted and smooth. Spread mixture over cooled brownies. Sprinkle with the remaining ½ cup pecans.

6 In a small saucepan heat and stir the remaining ¼ cup chocolate pieces over low heat until melted and smooth. Drizzle chocolate over the top of brownies. Let stand for 2 hours before serving.

7 Using the edges of the foil, lift the uncut brownies out of the pan; cut into bars.

PER SERVING 291 **CAL**; 18 g **FAT** (9 g **SAT**); 42 mg **CHOL**; 102 mg **SODIUM**; 33 g **CARB**; 2 g **FIBER**; 4 g **PRO**

Toffee Crackle Cookies

These crisp cookies, studded with bits of toffee, satisfy when you want just a bite of something sweet.

MAKES 48 servings **PREP** 25 minutes **BAKE** 20 minutes per batch at 300°F

1 cup butter, softened
1 cup packed brown sugar
1 teaspoon baking powder
¼ teaspoon salt
1 egg
1 teaspoon vanilla
2¼ cups all-purpose flour
1 cup chocolate-covered toffee pieces
Granulated sugar

1 Preheat oven to 300°F. In a large mixing bowl beat butter with an electric mixer on medium to high for 30 seconds. Add brown sugar, baking powder, and salt. Beat until combined, scraping sides of bowl occasionally. Beat in egg and vanilla until combined. Beat in as much of the flour as you can with the mixer. Using a wooden spoon, stir in any remaining flour. Stir in toffee pieces.

2 Shape dough into 1¼-inch balls. Place 2 inches apart on an ungreased cookie sheet. Dip the bottom of a glass in granulated sugar and flatten each ball to about ¼-inch thickness.

3 Bake for 20 minutes or until edges are firm but not brown. Transfer cookies to a wire rack; cool.

PER SERVING 109 **CAL**; 5 g **FAT** (3 g **SAT**); 16 mg **CHOL**; 76 mg **SODIUM**; 14 g **CARB**; 1 g **PRO**

Peanut Butter and Oatmeal Ice Cream Sandwiches

Make these magnificent ice cream sandwiches a day or two ahead of serving. Wrap each one tightly in plastic wrap, then store in a tightly sealed freezer bag for freshness.

MAKES 10 servings **PREP** 30 minutes **FREEZE** 1 hour **BAKE** 10 minutes per batch at 375°F

- **1** **quart vanilla ice cream, cut into 10 slices**
- **1** **quart chocolate ice cream, cut into 10 slices**
- **¾** **cup peanut butter**
- **½** **cup butter, softened**
- **¾** **cup packed brown sugar**
- **½** **cup granulated sugar**
- **½** **teaspoon baking powder**
- **¼** **teaspoon baking soda**
- **2** **eggs**
- **1** **teaspoon vanilla**
- **1¼** **cups all-purpose flour**
- **2½** **cups regular rolled oats**
- **1½** **cups raisins and/or semisweet chocolate pieces**

1 Line a baking pan or tray with waxed paper. Place the slices of vanilla and chocolate ice cream on the prepared pan. Cover with waxed paper; freeze for 1 hour.

2 Meanwhile, preheat oven to 375°F. In a large mixing bowl beat the peanut butter and butter with an electric mixer on medium to high for 30 seconds. Add the brown sugar, granulated sugar, baking powder, and baking soda. Beat on medium until fluffy. Add eggs and vanilla; beat well. Beat in flour on low. Using a wooden spoon, stir in oats and raisins.

3 Using ¼ cup dough for each cookie, drop dough 3 inches apart onto greased cookie sheets. Press the dough into 4 inch circles. (You should make 20 cookies.)

4 Bake for 10 minutes or until edges are golden. Let the cookies stand for 1 minute. Transfer cookies to wire racks; cool.

5 To assemble sandwiches, place one slice of vanilla and one slice of chocolate ice cream between two cookies.

PER SERVING 848 **CAL**; 36 g **FAT** (16 g **SAT**); 110 mg **CHOL**; 334 mg **SODIUM**; 117 g **CARB**; 9 g **FIBER**; 21 g **PRO**

Nutty Whiskey Ice Cream

Alissa Ward likes to make spiced nuts and often uses cayenne in her recipes. It might have been that or the whiskey in this super-creamy vanilla-bean ice cream studded with pecans that clinched her first-place win in the adult division of the 2013 Iowa Egg Council's Incredibly Good Eggs recipe contest. Either way, the mother of two young children and first-time recipe-contest competitor won an iPad mini.

MAKES 10 servings **PREP** 30 minutes **CHILL** 4 hours **BAKE** 4 minutes at 350°F **FREEZE** 4 hours

2½ **cups whipping cream**
1½ **cups whole milk**
¾ **cups sugar (12 tablespoons)**
¼ **teaspoon salt**
2 **vanilla beans**
8 **egg yolks**
½ **teaspoon ground cinnamon**
⅛ **teaspoon cayenne pepper**
½ **cup pecan pieces**
1 **tablespoon butter, melted**
1½ **teaspoons honey**
3 **tablespoons whiskey (such as Jameson Irish whiskey)**

1 In a medium saucepan combine whipping cream, 1 cup of the milk, 6 tablespoons of the sugar, and the salt. With a small knife, split the vanilla beans lengthwise and scrape seeds from beans. Add seeds and split beans to pan. Heat over medium-high heat. When mixture just begins to bubble around edges, remove from heat; cover and set aside. Remove vanilla beans and discard.

2 For the custard, in a medium bowl whisk together egg yolks and remaining sugar. Slowly whisk in 1 cup of the hot cream mixture; return cream mixture to saucepan. Cook over medium heat, stirring constantly, until custard thickens and coats the back of a spoon. Remove from heat and stir in remaining ½ cup milk.

3 Strain custard through a fine-mesh sieve into a bowl placed in a larger bowl of ice water. Stir custard until cooled. Cover and refrigerate until thoroughly chilled or up to 24 hours.

4 To prepare the nuts, preheat oven to 350°F. In a small bowl combine the cinnamon and cayenne pepper. Line a baking sheet with parchment paper. Toss the pecans with melted butter then spread in a thin layer on the prepared baking sheet. Drizzle honey over nuts and sprinkle with spice mixture. Gently stir to combine. Roast in the oven for 4 to 6 minutes, stirring once halfway through. Cool on a wire rack.

5 When ready to freeze the chilled custard, stir in whiskey. Freeze in a 4- to 5-quart ice cream freezer according to manufacturer's directions. Stir in seasoned pecans. Transfer ice cream to a 2-quart freezer container. Cover and freeze for at least 4 hours before serving.

PER SERVING 395 **CAL**; 32 g **FAT** (17 g **SAT**); 236 mg **CHOL**; 114 mg **SODIUM**; 21 g **CARB**; 1 g **FIBER**; 5 g **PRO**

Index

D

E

F

G

H–K

Metric Information

The charts on this page provide a guide for converting measurements from the U.S. customary system, which is used throughout this book, to the metric system.

PRODUCT DIFFERENCES

Most of the ingredients called for in the recipes in this book are available in most countries. However, some are known by different names. Here are some common American ingredients and their possible counterparts:

- Sugar (white) is granulated, fine granulated, or castor sugar.
- Confectioners' sugar is icing sugar.
- All-purpose flour is enriched, bleached or unbleached white household flour. When self-rising flour is used in place of all-purpose flour in a recipe that calls for leavening, omit the leavening agent (baking soda or baking powder) and salt.
- Light-color corn syrup is golden syrup.
- Cornstarch is cornflour.
- Baking soda is bicarbonate of soda.
- Vanilla or vanilla extract is vanilla essence.
- Green, red, or yellow sweet peppers are capsicums or bell peppers.
- Golden raisins are sultanas.

VOLUME AND WEIGHT

The United States traditionally uses cup measures for liquid and solid ingredients. The chart, top right, shows the approximate imperial and metric equivalents. If you are accustomed to weighing solid ingredients, the following approximate equivalents will be helpful.

- 1 cup butter, castor sugar, or rice = 8 ounces = ½ pound = 250 grams
- 1 cup flour = 4 ounces = ¼ pound = 125 grams
- 1 cup icing sugar = 5 ounces = 150 grams

Canadian and U.S. volume for a cup measure is 8 fluid ounces (237 ml), but the standard metric equivalent is 250 ml.

1 British imperial cup is 10 fluid ounces.

In Australia, 1 tablespoon equals 20 ml, and there are 4 teaspoons in the Australian tablespoon.

Spoon measures are used for smaller amounts of ingredients. Although the size of the tablespoon varies slightly in different countries, for practical purposes and for recipes in this book, a straight substitution is all that's necessary. Measurements made using cups or spoons always should be level unless stated otherwise.

COMMON WEIGHT RANGE REPLACEMENTS

Imperial/U.S.	Metric
½ ounce	15 g
1 ounce	25 g or 30 g
4 ounces (¼ pound)	115 g or 125 g
8 ounces (½ pound)	225 g or 250 g
16 ounces (1 pound)	450 g or 500 g
1¼ pounds	625 g
1½ pounds	750 g
2 pounds or 2¼ pounds	1,000 g or 1 Kg

OVEN TEMPERATURE EQUIVALENTS

Fahrenheit Setting	Celsius Setting*	Gas Setting
300°F	150°C	Gas Mark 2 (very low)
325°F	160°C	Gas Mark 3 (low)
350°F	180°C	Gas Mark 4 (moderate)
375°F	190°C	Gas Mark 5 (moderate)
400°F	200°C	Gas Mark 6 (hot)
425°F	220°C	Gas Mark 7 (hot)
450°F	230°C	Gas Mark 8 (very hot)
475°F	240°C	Gas Mark 9 (very hot)
500°F	260°C	Gas Mark 10 (extremely hot)
Broil	Broil	Grill

*Electric and gas ovens may be calibrated using celsius. However, for an electric oven, increase celsius setting 10 to 20 degrees when cooking above 160°C. For convection or forced air ovens (gas or electric) lower the temperature setting 25°F/10°C when cooking at all heat levels.

BAKING PAN SIZES

Imperial/U.S.	Metric
9x1½-inch round cake pan	22- or 23x4-cm (1.5 L)
9x1½-inch pie plate	22- or 23x4-cm (1 L)
8x8x2-inch square cake pan	20x5-cm (2 L)
9x9x2-inch square cake pan	22- or 23x4.5-cm (2.5 L)
11x7x1½-inch baking pan	28x17x4-cm (2 L)
2-quart rectangular baking pan	30x19x4.5-cm (3 L)
13x9x2-inch baking pan	34x22x4.5-cm (3.5 L)
15x10x1-inch jelly roll pan	40x25x2-cm
9x5x3-inch loaf pan	23x13x8-cm (2 L)
2-quart casserole	2 L

U.S./STANDARD METRIC EQUIVALENTS

⅛ teaspoon = 0.5 ml	⅓ cup = 3 fluid ounces = 75 ml
¼ teaspoon = 1 ml	½ cup = 4 fluid ounces = 125 ml
½ teaspoon = 2 ml	⅔ cup = 5 fluid ounces = 150 ml
1 teaspoon = 5 ml	¾ cup = 6 fluid ounces = 175 ml
1 tablespoon = 15 ml	1 cup = 8 fluid ounces = 250 ml
2 tablespoons = 25 ml	2 cups = 1 pint = 500 ml
¼ cup = 2 fluid ounces = 50 ml	1 quart = 1 litre